How to Become the Most Successful Millennial in Your Organisation

By
Gerard Bissett

Copyright © 2017 Gerard Bissett
All rights reserved.

ISBN-13:978-1543242287

ISBN-10:1543242286

DEDICATION

This Book is dedicated to my mother Gráinne who has scarified so much for me. Everything you do is to help me in some way. There's no way that I could ever thank you, I just hope that I make you proud. From the fivers at the bottom of the stairs, to the food on the table. You've been the greatest mother in the world, I am blessed beyond belief. Thank you God, for giving me such an amazing mother. Thank you for allowing me to follow my dreams and for believing in me.

Table of Contents

Foreword: Fire from the Dragons Mouth by Gavin Duffy — Pg 6

Introduction: Why Read This Book? — Pg 8

Chapter 1: The Bulletproof Mentality — Pg 13

Chapter 2: Do You Want It? Go Get It! — Pg 29

Chapter 3: How to Become a World class Communicator — Pg 47

Chapter 4: The Millennial Leader — Pg 60

Chapter 5: Teamwork Makes the Dream Work — Pg 73

Chapter 6: What Time is it? — Pg 87

Chapter 7: How to Stay Engaged at Work — Pg 98

Chapter 8: How to Rise to the Top — Pg 112

Chapter 9: DE Stress for More Success   Pg 126

Chapter 10: Crafting Your Dream Career   Pg 140

Conclusion: Top Golden Nuggets from   Pg 151
the Book

Foreword
Fire from the Dragon's Mouth

As a successful businessman and one of the Dragon's on RTE's television show *Dragons' Den*, I am an expert on analysing, advising and investing in businesses. I highly recommend this book because it sets forth specific strategies for how millennials can enhance their performance in the workplace. This book is written by Gerard Bissett, an Irish millennial, focuses on helping millennials overcome a variety of challenges that they commonly face in the workplace.

Gerard's book is not only a must-read for millennials but also one for those managers and executives who work with millennials, as it offers them a guide for training and enhancing the performance of their millennial workforce.

When Gerard asked me to write the foreword for *How to Become the Most Successful Millennial in Your Organization,* I was happy to do so. I greatly admire the millennial generation for the challenging times they've witnessed growing up. When I first met Gerard in 2015, he immediately struck me as a charismatic, confident, and enlightened young man.

You probably listen to Gerard's podcasts. On the episode Gerard and I recorded together, I advise millennials not to limit themselves to a job title. I regularly meet people, and they say "Oh I am an accountant" or "I am a plumber." This does little for me. Whereas if someone says to me "Hi Gavin, I can help you save money on your taxes." It catches my attention much better. So, find a way that you can stand out from the crowd. In a world of Hi-tech be Hi-touch.

As a Dragon, on Dragons' Den I am fortunate to have met and worked with some outstanding entrepreneurs. I am proud to say that I am a huge advocate of enterprise here in Ireland, and love help business in any way that I can. Be it investing on the Den or being a founding member of organisations such as the Irish Chapter of EO, the International Entrepreneur's Organisation. However, when it comes to employing people, I look to employ millennials.

As you embark on this journey, I want to leave you with the following quote.

"The only way to do great work is to love what you do. If you haven't found it yet, keep looking. Don't settle. As with all matters of the heart, you'll know when you find it." – Steve Jobs.

Gavin Duffy - 2017
Entrepreneur, Investor.

Introduction

"Tell me and I forget. Teach me and I may remember. Involve me and I learn."
-Ben Franklin

Do you know what time it is? It's time that you start learning *How to Become the Most Successful Millennial in Your Organisation*. How would this make you feel? You and I are about to embark on a journey together. From this moment forward we are striving towards achieving our goals. Beware, this book will open your mind to what is possible when you dare to live your dreams. I think you'll be shocked by what you're about to read. This book holds many of those "I wish I knew this sooner" moments.

Let's be honest. You already have what it takes to win. Now is the time to dig deep to discover what's been holding you back, and remove any mental blocks to your success. Achieving success in any organisation is no easy task, but this book will show you exactly how to do it. You'll finish this book with a strategic plan gearing you towards your success. You hold in your hand a blueprint for achievement, which opens the way to life-enriching opportunities. This book will empower you with vital insights to program your subconscious mind to achieve whatever it is you want. It's time to discover your hidden talents, develop self-confidence, set goals, and start to unlock your potential. My goal of this book is to awaken your spirit to take the first step towards a fulfilling, successful career. Imagine the possibilities! Only you hold the key to your success, this book is merely a tool to help you achieve more in less time.

I've done the research and discovered the key challenges of the workplace, and the skills you need to overcome them. Take a lesson from the superstars. You are going to learn Bill Gates secret to success. You'll learn how Steve Jobs unleashed his creativity, and discover Barack Obama's secret to decision making. You'll also learn an NFL player's strategy to bounce back when life got him down, and his original goal setting technique. If you commit to staying with me and read this book to the end, I promise to deliver on your expectations. If I'm going to promise you something, I expect something small in return. That is, you will not let your learning from this book lead to more knowledge. Instead, you'll let your knowledge lead to action.

Why listen to me?
The main reason you should listen to me is that my primary interest is helping you achieve what you want from life. For almost ten years I have been obsessed with discovering how ordinary people from all walks of life became successful. I've read hundreds of books and learned how the best become the best. I've got a very successful podcast show interviewing New York Times

bestselling authors, super bowl champions, and industry experts alike. I've even written some books myself. I'm regularly invited to speak in organisations. I'm also well educated, I've an honours degree in business and was one of the top performing students in my class. I've had the pleasure of consulting companies from boutique elder law firms in the US to the local butcher in Ireland. Everything that I've learned through these experiences is in this book.

Too many people don't chase their dreams and live with regret. I didn't want that to be me, that is why I took the time out of my life to write this book. Not for me, I did it for you. I want this book to stand for something and be meaningful in your life. My goal for this book is for one person to become successful in their organisation, and for them to help just one person do the same. If we all just helped each other soon we would impact the nation, and if we impact the nation we can change the world.

Will this book make me rich? As an act of contribution, I have decided to donate a part of the proceeds to charity. Therefore, purchasing this book will not only help you, but it will also help many others. So please pass the word on to your friends and family.

What's in it for you?
This book gives you permission to succeed when others say that you can't. I believe in you, even if you don't believe in yourself. But sometimes you

just got to believe in someone else's belief in you, before the belief in yourself kicks in.

Each chapter tackles a challenge that you will face along the way. Let me take you through the process in steps.

First things first, you will learn how to develop the mental toughness you need to succeed. It's time to wake up the warrior inside of you.

You've dreamed about it. Now you can do it! This book guides you step by step so that you can achieve virtually any goal you envision.

What's a fundamental workplace challenge? You guessed it! Communication skills. You will learn my exact process I use for delivering presentations, and how to leave an impact on the audience.

This book gives you permission to lead, not follow. Wait until you discover my leadership formula that every great leader enacts.

There will be no problem that you can't solve, as I guide you through the step by step process that world class organisations use to solve problems.

Teamwork will now be a pleasurable experience. You'll no longer feel that you're doing all the work as you learn the secret to getting full commitment from team members.

Do you procrastinate from time to time? Well not anymore. Do you feel like you could be getting more done in a day than you currently achieve? It's time to make the leap into the world of time mastery. This book helps you leverage time so that you have the time for the things that matter in life.

That's not all! This book lays out practical tips and strategies that will make you not only the most successful in your organisation, but also the most valuable.

I think it's fair to say that sometimes we might find ourselves in stressful scenarios. Maybe a problem that you can't solve, an ongoing issue with a co-worker, or maybe something in your personal life. This book shows you have you can remove those stressful situations by identifying what's causing the stress, then a strategy to overcome it.

Lastly, this book would not be complete unless you had the tools to get the job you want. Learn why your current résumé is useless. Why asking for a seven-figure salary during your initial interview for an entry-level job is a good idea. How you can build your personal brand to use as your greatest tool, and how to make the most of career fairs.

Chapter 1
The Bulletproof Mentality

"Whether you think you can or you think you can't, you're right."
- Henry Ford

I'm just like you, I have goals, and like you, I know that I'm capable of more than I'm currently achieving. I want this chapter to broaden your perspective and open your mind to how a simple shift in your mindset can be the difference between success and failure.

This whole journey started for me when I was 13 years old. I knew that I wanted to help people I just wasn't sure how. One summer while on holidays in Spain with my uncle Thomas I had a radical shift in my mindset, I had been exposed to personal development. I knew then that this was my vehicle to help people. I believed that everyone had the right to know what I had learned. I went back to school after the summer holidays, and instantly my grades started to improve. I was far from perfect, and it wasn't until I went to college that I started to succeed within education. The lessons that I learned in Spain changed my life forever. I developed the attitude that I could have anything that I want, once I put my mind to it. All this success talk made me hungry to start my own business, so that's exactly what I did. I was visiting with my uncle Thomas when we came up with the idea that I would start a grass cutting business.

I was just a kid, and I had no money to buy a lawnmower. How would I start this business? We figured that I would save up my pocket money and buy a used lawnmower. To me, that was going to take too much time. I was so hungry for success, so I started asking friends and family that when I got my mower could I cut their grass. From the offset, I had received tremendous support. I knew I had to do something, so I went to the local hire store and hired a lawnmower. On that day "Gerry's Services" was born. I had a website, business cards, pens, t-shirts, everything you would expect a company to have, and I was just 13.

I immediately started getting attention for how professional I was and began to build up a client base quickly. I had a trailer that I would attach to the back of my bicycle filled with my equipment. My uncle Derek had allowed me to store all my equipment in his yard. I would usually start around 10am and finish in the afternoon, and then I would go into Derek's house for tea and a snack. I learned so much about business from Derek, and he told me to just stick to the grass because that's where the money was. He was right. I burned myself out by taking on too many projects, and I hit a mental barrier. Here's what I did to turn things back around.

You Decide

You already have what it takes to succeed. You just need to challenge yourself. I read books, listen to audios, and sometimes I don't apply what I have learned. There's one thing however that I've learned that has always stuck with me.

Every morning when I wake up, I believe that I have two choices. Option one is that I can be in a bad mood. Bad moods may consist of complaining and reacting to everything that will happen to me during the day. What good will this do me? None. Life is too short to be in a bad humour. Option two is that I can wake up and decide to be in a good mood. What a great way to start the day! This is when you get excited about the day ahead, and you don't let things bother you because you know they're outside of your control. I always thought this was an interesting way to start the day so I shared it with my local butcher a few years back.

Then one day I was in his shop when he said, "There's one thing that I have learned from you."

My response was, "There should be more than one thing you've learned from me, but go on what is it?"

He said, "When I wake up in the morning I have two choices, to be in a good mood or be in a bad mood."

I was delighted that he'd learned that from me.

I'm also delighted to share it with you because it's a principle I live my life by.

When you realise that your mood and feelings are conscious decisions you make, your whole life begins to change. So, start every day by putting yourself in a positive state. I find tremendous value in having a morning ritual and taking part of the morning to fill the mind with positivity. Find something that works for you. This state will continue throughout the day. If you're going to be thinking, it may as well be positive.

Get Clear on Mindset

Have you ever wondered what kind of mindset will make you a successful millennial? According to Harvard Business Review, if you work for a company with a growth mindset, you're 34% more likely to feel a greater sense of ownership and commitment to the company. You're also more likely to get hired internally, that's good news! Growth company employees are also 47% more likely to say that their colleagues are trustworthy.

Carol Dweck, a Stanford professor, is the author of the book *Mindset*. She proposes a theory that there are two types of mindsets that people have. The first is the fixed mindset, these are the kind of people that criticise and envy the success of others, and believe that intelligence is fixed. Do you know any of these people? I know I do. The second is the growth mindset, and it's my belief that this is the kind of mindset you need to have to be successful. Why? Because these are the kind of people, who embrace challenges and love to learn. They believe that there's no such thing as failure, only feedback. They use failure as a learning curve in the pursuit of their next challenge.

I want you to ask yourself, what kind of mindset do you have?

With this is mind it's clear to see how getting your head right will help you excel in the workplace.

I learned recently from my podcast guest Philip McKernan that mindset is overrated and we need to get out of our heads. What Philip says is that we need to focus on our soul set. What this means is that we go with our gut feelings and intuition. He says there's no five-step process, it's inside us all, it's our gift. Follow your gut and don't let anybody tell you that you can't do something.

How to Eliminate Self-Doubt

Two voices are talking in your head. One of them is saying that you can do it, the other says that you can't. One voice tells you that you aren't good enough, you don't have the talent, you don't have the time, nobody likes you anyway, or you don't have the resources. This type of negative thinking is irrational, yet somehow we manage to convince ourselves that it's true. It's so much easier to be negative and list the reasons why we can't succeed. We give ourselves an out and justify not even trying. I'm just like you I'm guilty of this too, we all are, but now let's make a change.

I once had the privilege to see Jack Canfield speak in Dublin. The most important point that I took from his presentation was to create a list of 200 reasons why you CAN succeed.

I'm not aware of a way to eliminate negative thinking. Some things work for me that I'll share with you. I believe that firstly we must learn to change the internal dialogue that goes on in our heads. Stop telling yourself the negative story and tell yourself an empowering story. Many people say "But the story I tell myself is the truth." Yes, that may be true, but if the story you are telling yourself isn't empowering you, it's the wrong story.

When experiencing self-doubt ask yourself this question.

What way would a successful person think in this situation?

Often this self-doubt can be triggered by other people. I hear so often about people doubting themselves because of someone else, that thinks whatever they're doing is not a good idea. A lot of the time what this person is saying is that they can't do it and if you tried and succeeded they'd be jealous. Therefore, they knock your confidence and make you believe the voice in your head that says you can't succeed.

Would you like to know how to deal with these people? Good! There are two options. First, you cut them out of your life. You don't need this type of person in your life anyway. Second, results! You approach them and say, "You don't believe in me. That's ok because I believe in myself. I'm going to give this shot, and in five years one of us is going to be right. Either I'm a huge success or a complete failure."

Then you must go out there and do whatever it takes to prove yourself right, and prove them wrong. Bye Bye, with doubting yourself.

Believe in Yourself

When I was a kid one of the most exciting times for me was Christmas. I always looked forward to waking up on Christmas morning and playing with my toys. I spent many Christmases in the Canary Islands as a child. So, yeah I used to go swimming on Christmas Day. I remember one Christmas Eve I was standing on the balcony of our hotel room, and my mother tells me she sees Santa's sleigh.
I was like "No way, Mam where?"
She says "Look up and to the left."
I swear on my life, clear as day, on that night I also saw Santa's sleigh. My mother was clearly joking with me, but in my mind, it was so real. I wanted

to share this story because it illustrates how strong our beliefs can be.

Have you ever seen that quote, "If you can believe in Santa for ten years, you can believe in yourself for 10 minutes." It's sad that we do not believe in ourselves because when we do the magic starts to happen.

Just like self-doubt, the wrong belief system can have negative implications. Let's say for example that there's a promotion coming up in your organisation, and your first thought is, "What's the point of even applying. I'm not good enough for that position anyway."
Whereas the successful person looks and says, "Wow I'm going to grab that opportunity by the horns."
Who do you think gets the promotion? Here's my belief, if you do not believe in yourself, then who will? I encourage you that when you see opportunity that you capitalise on it, and believe you have what it takes to follow it through.

Did you know that when you are working towards a goal or learning new things that it strengthens your brain? This is called neuroplasticity. It's how our brains translate information from the external environment, and how it impacts the thoughts we think. The point I want to get across here is the power of your mind and belief system.

Maybe a story will put it into a greater perspective.

Let me tell you the story of the man who found an eagle egg, and put it in a barnyard under a chicken. Eventually, the eagle egg hatched, and he grew up with the baby chicks. Every day the eagle did the same things as the chickens. Until one day the eagle was looking up into the sky and saw another eagle flying high, and through the wind doing tumbles, twists, and dives.

He asked his friend, "Hey what kind of bird is that up there?"

His friend replied, "Wow I'm not sure."

The eagle proceeded to say, "I sure wish I could fly like that."

What do you think was holding this eagle back? His beliefs of course. He had a limiting belief that he could not do what the eagle in the sky was doing. You and I both know that this was not the case and that he could. Therefore, it's important to identify our limiting beliefs and challenge them, instead of accepting them as truth. My question is, will you let your beliefs hold you back?

Albert Einstein had an excellent quote, "Everybody is a genius. But if you judge a fish by its ability to climb a tree, it will live its whole life believing it is stupid."

The Attitude of Winners

Have you ever looked at somebody and thought, wow they have a great attitude? It's time for you to become that person! I haven't always had the same attitude I have now, but when I adopted this kind of attitude into my life, my results skyrocketed. The good news is the same is about to happen for you, stay with me on this.

Let me tell you a little story. Two salesmen were traveling to Africa to do market research for the launch of a new shoe company.

After the first day one of the salesmen calls his boss and says, "Hey boss, I'm coming home. There are no opportunities here. Nobody wears any shoes."
His boss agreed, and he was on the next plane home.
On the same day, the second salesman also calls his boss and says, "Hey boss I'm coming home, I've got all the information I need. There's opportunity everywhere because nobody is wearing any shoes. We can sell to the whole country."

His boss was delighted. Now let's imagine that you were the second salesman with that kind of attitude. What do you think this will do for your success? This is the kind of attitude organisations look for, not just in millennials, but in everybody. Just think of the many opportunities for promotion, the size of your bonus, and the impact you can have, with that type of attitude.

I believe that it's the little things that make the big difference. Negative thinkers will see difficulties in every opportunity, whereas positive thinkers see opportunity in every difficulty. Isn't that what happened in the story? One sales guy spotted an opportunity when the other spotted a problem. The choice is yours. I always try to remind myself that truly successful people have a positive attitude, and if it's good enough for them, it's good enough for me.

Another story I believe captures a fantastic attitude is as follows. A man is walking on the beach at low tide, and the beach is covered in starfish that are still alive but will die soon. The man starts to throw them back into the sea one by one.

An onlooker see's the man and says, "What are you doing? There is no way you can save all these starfish. There are hundreds of them, what difference will it make?"
The man continued and remained silent as the onlooker got closer when the man replied, "It will make a difference to that one right there." As he threw another starfish back into the water.

I don't know about you, but one thing is for certain, and that's, I hate being around people with a negative attitude. The research tells us that we become the average of the five people we spend the most time with. So, if three of your friends smoke crack cocaine? Guess what? You are the perfect candidate to start smoking crack. Whereas, if three of your friends are millionaires or the highest performers in their organisation, there's a good chance their behaviour's and attitude will rub off on you. What do you think happens when you pick up their habits? That's right, you guessed it, you will begin to replicate or experience similar results. I hope this encourages you to have a winning attitude towards your potential, and that you can do anything with the right attitude. Always remember, have an attitude of gratitude.

If You Don't Know Yourself, Who does?

If you are a millennial and you are striving toward success, you may be familiar with a guy called Gary Vaynerchuck or Gary Vee. Gary Vee says that the most important skill you can have in the world is self-awareness. Some of us are so unaware of what is happening around us that it's scary to think of the consequences. Self-awareness, in a nutshell, is that you are aware of your surroundings. You're also aware of your strengths and weaknesses; what you can and can't do. You may even have a list of the areas that you need to improve upon and use personal growth strategies to help you do that. The people who are really self-aware, recognise some of their bad habits and will take actions to erase them. Meditating helps us become more self-aware, writing down what it is we want to achieve, and asking ourselves questions. Such as, why we do, what we do? This will also give you a compelling future you can strive towards, and achieve. When you know yourself, you know exactly where you fit in, in your organisation. You will learn more about this as you continue reading the book.

Emotional intelligence or EQ is a hot topic these days. I like Tony Robbin's analogy better, that is we need to be emotionally fit. This means that you control your emotions and not the other way around. When we have this kind of power, just imagine the possibilities. Even an emotionally fit person will still experience negative emotions, the key is not to let them live in your mind. When feeling down or depressed, the emotionally fit person realises that they need a radical shift in their body to put them back into their power state. Not only is this an instant change in our mood, but it also increases our focus and motivation. Use emotional fitness to be in control of your emotions. It's this kind of power that will put you in charge of your destiny to become the most successful millennial in your organisation.

If You're Not Growing, You're Dying

I'm an Irish guy, the food we eat is pretty bland, to say the least. During my time in Florida, I made a decision that when I was there, I was going to be open minded and try new foods. You see in Ireland I had some kind of fear about trying new food, whereas in the States I didn't have the same fear. I have no problem stepping outside of my comfort zone. I was once in a Latino bar and got up on the stage and sang in Spanish (True story). How's that for stepping outside my comfort zone? However, when it came to food and exercise that was not the case, I had a little comfort zone that I was perfectly happy to remain inside it. I decided that I was going to try new things. I started by eating Vietnamese food with my cousin Kevin at a restaurant we went to, and I loved it. Then we went to a Mexican restaurant where I also fell in love with their food. I think if I didn't it would be an insult, considering I'm an affluent Spanish speaker. I then had to step outside of my comfort zone with some exercise. I decided to try Yoga and found it excellent. It was such a mind opening experience and brought me great peace of mind, not to mention the health benefits. The point I'm trying to illustrate here is that some of the best things that ever happened in my life were when I faced some kind of fear within my own little comfort zone. As soon as I stepped outside of that ballpark, magic truly started to happen in my life. Grow, grow, grow!

Self Control

Have you ever noticed how the people who do the most complaining in the world are always the ones who never take any responsibility? They will fight you to the end just to prove their point and irritate everybody around them in the process. To me, self-control is when we oversee our emotions, not our emotions overseeing us. Do your emotions control you or do you control your emotions? Certain things in life are outside of our control. That's ok, let it go, do not waste time and energy on what's out of your control. Take time each day to relax and focus on yourself, over time you will unlock your true potential.

Ask yourself what do you need to control? Is it what you're eating? Is it something you're doing that you shouldn't? When you've figured this out, and you feel yourself itching to do whatever it is you shouldn't do, ride the wave. Give yourself 10 minutes before given in. Usually, this is enough time for the desire to pass. If you give in, it's no big deal. However, don't spend time in self-guilt, forgive yourself quickly and move on. Shift your focus on improving so that you don't give in the next time.

How to Stay Motivated

Have you ever heard the phrase by Zig Ziglar, "People say motivation doesn't last. Well, neither does bathing, that's why we recommend it daily." As people, we are motivated by different things, so being self-motivated comes from when you are truly inspired by something. Being truly inspired can take some soul searching, but when you find it, I promise you'll be super motivated. You'll know when you've found it because the pursuit becomes meaningful, it's your purpose.

The thing is, you are already motivated, and if you think, "Oh well I am not motivated to do XYZ." You and I both know this isn't true, we also know that if we're doing something incredibly important to us, we don't need motivation.

All of us are motivated, some people are motivated to wake up every morning and go to the gym, others are motivated to stay at home on the couch all day. Some people seem to use money as a motivator. This doesn't work long term. The research suggests that incentives such as money, only act as a motivator when we must perform tasks that are straightforward. This is because incentives narrow our focus and enable us to put our head down. When we must perform more complex tasks, the higher the incentive, the pooper our ability to carry out the work. This is called the distraction effect as the brain gets distracted by the economic reward and the task at hand.

I'm not sure who said it first, but I love this parable. When the archer shoots for nothing, he has all his skills. When he shoots for a brass buckle, he is already nervous. When he shoots for a prize of gold, he is blind or sees two targets. His skills haven't changed, but the prize divides him. He thinks more of winning than he does of shooting, and the need to win drains him of his power.

The key to staying motivated is doing things for the love of your craft!

Chapter 2
Do You Want it? Go Get it!

"If you want to live a happy life, tie it to a goal. Not to people or things."
-Albert Einstein

What I find interesting, is that Harvard MBA graduates were asked if they had goals and plans to accomplish them. The replies of the graduates showed: 84% had no specific goals, 13% had goals, but not committed to paper, and the remaining 3% had clear written goals and planned to accomplish them. I hope you're reading this sitting down, because of those 13% who had goals, they on average earned twice as much as the remaining 84% who had no goals. What is even more staggering is that the 3% who had clear goals clearly written down, earned on average ten times the amount of the remaining 97% of the graduates.

Studies also show that when we've our goals written down, we have an 80% greater chance of achieving them. I also saw a Facebook post that said we are 1100% times more likely to achieve our goals when we write them down. I think it's best to stick with the 80%.

I could not write this book without guiding you through the goal setting process. The chapter on mindset is to get your head right so that you can start to set some goals. You've seen the statistics from Harvard. Now you need to make sure that you set your goals accordingly. I recommend going onto my YouTube channel or iTunes and listen to the podcast I did with Setema Gali. This guy knows how to set some goals, going from winning the Super Bowl with the New England Patriots to growing a massive real estate empire. He then lost it all during the crash and made another go at it in the coaching industry. He talks about having what the legendary Jim Rohn called The BHAG which stands for Big Hairy Audacious Goals. Another technique that is widely popular is the SMART approach. An acronym which stands for specific, measurable, attainable, realistic, and timed. Later in the chapter we'll get to my very own goals setting method.

I have many great ideas on what it takes to achieve your goals, and since I'm a nice guy, I'll share them with you. As millennials, it's not about the money for this generation. I would still recommend you set financial goals and make some extra money so that you can anticipate the unexpected. But money is not everything. I believe having goals for every area of your life is important.

Are you familiar with Eric Thomas? He is an outstanding motivational speaker. I once watched a video on YouTube of him speaking where he tells a story of a guru. There was this guy, and he wanted to learn from the guru about how to be successful. The guru happily obliged to help him. The guru had one condition that the guy would meet him at the beach the following morning at 4:30 am. The guy agreed and arrived the next morning all pumped up and wearing a business suit.

The guru said, "Why are you wearing a suit to the beach?"

The guy said, "I'm here to be successful!"

"Ok," said the guru.

He asked the guy to walk out into the water. The guy thought it was strange, but did it anyway. He walked out up to his waist, but the guru told him to keep going.

Eventually, the guy got up to his neck and said, "I can't go any further."

"Keep going." Replied the guru.

"If I go any further I won't be able to breathe." The guy told the guru.

Then there was a sudden pause as the guru said, "When you want to succeed as bad as you want to breathe, then you will be successful."

How compelling is that story? What are you willing to do to achieve your goals?

Find Your Why, and You're Halfway There

When I was about 14, I watched a TEDx talk by Simon Sinex entitled, "How Great Leaders Inspire Action." If you haven't looked at this video I highly recommend that you do so, it's available on YouTube. The whole reasoning behind the video is that what we do is really of little importance versus why we do what we do. So why not start with why? This video got me so excited that I just wanted to share it with a like-minded individual, so I sent it to my cousin Kevin. At the time, he probably thought what does this kid know. It was not until a couple of years later when he was at a seminar and one of the speakers said everybody ought to check out this video. Then he knew I was on to something.

So, let's start with why? I know what my why is, my question is, what is yours? You may be interested to know that part of my why, is helping you find yours. As I come from extremely humble beginnings, my why is to contribute and serve my mother in any way that I can, and have her proud to say I'm her son. I hope that I am doing a good job, but I am wise enough to know there's always room for improvement.

Finding your why can be tough sometimes, especially when dealing with uncertainty. In his book *Start With Why*, Sinex writes about the US flag, and how it's a representation of the country's beliefs and values. The flag is so powerful that US soldiers follow the flag into battle. Why? Because the set of values it portrays are important to every soldier, who wears the flag on their uniform. Have you ever considered what's important to you? This will help you dive deep and discover your why. However, if this does not help, there are some more questions you can ask yourself that make it a little easier along the way. The magic questions are.

Is this pursuit meaningful to me?
Am I staying true to my core beliefs and values?
Will my current path fulfil me?

If you ask yourself these questions, you will come up with some interesting answers. Taking the time to discover those answers will be some of the most valuable time spent in the world.

Create a Compelling Vision

"If you are working on something exciting that you really care about, you don't have to be pushed. The vision pulls you." -Steve Jobs

I could quote successful person after successful person, and I guarantee almost all of them started with a compelling vision. I've got a vision for my life regarding where I want to be in the future. I believe that without a vision it's easy to get stuck in the rat race and follow a road that will not fulfil you. Read the quote above. This quote has inspired me several times, mainly because of how true it is. A daily dose of inspiration is much better than a daily dose of cocaine. To me having a vision is about knowing what your ideal outcome looks like before you arrive at that destination. You can have a vision for just about anything, and you should have a vision for several things.

First, your relationships; without a vision, they become boring and on the road to nowhere.

Second, a vision for your health; you would be wrong to assume that you can get away with not taking care of yourself.

Third your finances; in the 21st century becoming financially secure is a must, having seen the effects of the 2008 recession.

Here's the catch, your vision will not happen unless you make it your business to make it happen. This immediately puts people on hold as the excuses rise to the surface. In the beginning, successful people have also made excuses such as; I don't have the time or the energy, I'm not smart enough, or there are too many competitors, I'm broke, and I could never find the money. These are called limiting beliefs and relate to what we have already discussed. Challenge them! You can make excuses or get results, not both.

Always remember that, when in the pursuit of fulfilling your vision there's no such thing as a lack of anything, you have just got to be more resourceful. Use images of the things you want in your life and put them together in a collage, look at it every day and see yourself as having already got there. Now plan what you are going to do to achieve it. Let the vision pull you!

I'll Hold You to It

A couple of years back I was at a conference in Dublin where I heard one of the best goal setting

strategies I have ever heard in my life. It's the concept of accountability. What this means is that as soon as you have decided what your goal is, the next step is to find three people who are important to you to hold you accountable to your goal. The reason why these people must be important to you, and not just any Tom, Dick, or Harry is because you must be disappointed to let them down. They can be your parents, best friend, favourite uncle or cousin, even your girlfriend or boyfriend. The key is that you will be disappointed if you let them down. When you know who they are you are going to call them, tell them your goal, and ask them a simple question.
"Will you hold me accountable to my goal and follow up with me to make sure I'm taking the relevant actions, and following through to achieve my goal?"
This way when they will call you and ask, "Where are you with your goals?" "What is this week's progress report?"
When you are asked these questions, and you don't have a progress update for them, these people will be disappointed in you. Imagine this person is your grandmother, you will be disappointed in yourself that you let her down. When you have this accountability factor, it will inspire you to take action and follow through on your goals. Gary Vaynerchuk also talks about accountability, and he attributes his fitness success to it. Can you imagine how much more you will achieve from being held accountable? By

taking responsibility for our actions, we craft ourselves into the best version of ourselves. Finally, the last part of accountability is the social element. If you wish, you can post and share your goals on social media, so that your peers can hold you accountable. Most people have a couple of hundred virtual friends, that is a lot of people knowing your commitment to your goals.

Let's use a weight loss goal as an example. You may post something like, "I'm sick and tired of weighing 200 pounds, six months from now on June 17th, I will weight 150 pounds." Putting it out there to the world makes it much more likely that you will follow through. I will also hold you accountable to some of your goals, connect with our Facebook group and share your goals with the incredibly supportive community.

If I'm going to hold you accountable to your goals, don't you think I deserve the same from you? Earlier today I was out cycling my bike when I had an idea. I figured that I should share some of my goals with you in this book. Why? Because maybe one of you reading this book could help me achieve them.

1. Be on the Late Late Show.
2. Become a New York Times bestselling author.
3. Interview A-list celebrities for my podcast. Such as Richard Branson, Arnold Schwarzenegger, Tony Robbins, Conor McGregor, The Rock, and Will Smith.
4. Be featured in a music video with a Latin pop artist. Such as Shakira or Enrique Iglesias.
5. Make $1,000,000 after taxes a year by living my passion.
6. Travel the world and experience all life has to offer.
7. Break a World Record.
8. Go to space.
9. Learn how to fly an airplane.
10. Be happy ☺ #Completed

Be Resilient

As you might imagine those who are successful are those who never gave up. When I was in school one of the teachers approached me, and asked if would considering coming up with a business idea that could be entered into the student enterprise competition. At the time, I had a couple of business ideas circulating in my head. One was creating a coconut shampoo product and using Network Marketing as a business model. I approached my teacher, and he thought it was a terrible idea and that I could be more creative. Some other students also had business ideas. The school liaison officer for the programme was due to come to our school that week to meet with us students to talk about the competition.

To be selected for the programme we needed to have our ideas ready before we met with the liaison officer. By this time, I had come up with the idea for a vending machine in the school that dispensed stationary instead of confectionary.

Finally, the day of the meeting had arrived, two other students and I were in a room with this lady discussing our ideas. One guy had an idea to develop an app to help students with their studies, and the other guy had an idea for a school bag that didn't feel heavy on your back. Each equally good ideas and relatively simple to execute. The objective of the programme was to come up with a well thought out business plan, and a prototype of your product or service. A challenge yes, but not an impossible objective to juggle while studying for exams.

My idea would be the most expensive to implement, but I was determined to do it anyway. When it came to it, the other two guys didn't have the tenacity to follow through on their ideas, and they gave up at the first hurdle. I, on the other hand, was just getting started. I decided that purchasing a vending machine was not practical, so I was going to lease one. By doing some research I found a guy close by that was willing to lease me a machine. He came by the school, and we signed the lease agreement and agreed on a monthly fee. The machine was due to be delivered the following Tuesday. On Monday evening, I received a call to say that he had to postpone a week due to a technical difficulty. That was ok. It gave me more time to prepare what I needed to get done.

This guy strung me along for weeks and weeks, with no sign of the machine being delivered. Then one day he called me to say that our deal was off. It looked like the whole project was going to fall apart as leasing a machine was the most practical solution, and this was the only company willing to work with me. I didn't have enough money to buy a machine.

    As luck would have it, one day I was browsing the internet when I came across a more suitable machine at a more affordable cost. I called the company right away and arranged a time to purchase the machine. It was a Thursday, and I took the day off school to purchase the machine with my uncle Derek. He's always a wonderful person to bring when you are purchasing something. He could write a book about negotiating the price. He saved me a lot of money on that day. I remember clear as day going through the drive thru at Burger King with my new vending machine in the back of Derek's jeep. I was excited about what was coming.

    Eventually, I had the machine installed at

my school with the help of the woodwork teacher. The next day was my first day in business. I made €17 and felt exhilarated.

Now for the student enterprise competition. I always liked to do things professionally so I had a t-shirt with my logo on it, and a cardboard cut out of the machine. My display looked pretty good. I became the first student ever from my school to participate in the competition. My machine had considerable interest from the judges, but I didn't win any prizes. The day was still a success because against the odds I had achieved something, and I didn't give up.

Everyone knows that action is the key to all success, yet most people never take the actions required to achieve their goals. I believe the biggest reason for this is self-doubt and fear of failure. I'm here to tell you that failure is nothing to be afraid of, success is what you really fear. I want to make sure this doesn't happen to you, and it doesn't hold you back from achieving your goals.

It's true that sometimes you must fall seven times so that you can stand up eight, my goal is to make it a little easier for you. I believe that sometimes fear is excitement in disguise. So, feel the fear and do it anyway.

When you've overcome this fear, the next step is to be resilient. What is resilience? Simply put it means never giving up no matter what, this will be the key to all your success.

Now, I want to share insights how you can develop resilience in pursuing your goals. When I wrote this book, I had no idea if it was going to be a success or not. I just knew that deep inside me I had to write it, or it would be something that I would regret.

That's the first step in being resilient, is realising that the pain of regret is always much greater than the pain of the challenge.

Step number two, if you've learned something, you haven't failed. One of the best nuggets I've ever learned is that there's no such thing as failure only feedback. What this means is that when you fail, you've figured out a way how not to do something. This also means you're a step closer to figuring it out.

Bill Gates said it much better than I ever could, "It's fine to celebrate success, but it is more important to heed the lessons of failure."

He also has another quote I believe adds value here, "Success is a lousy teacher. It seduces smart people into thinking they can't lose." – Bill Gates

It's ok to fail. You'll learn something, now try harder next time. The best thing about being resilient is that each time you try, you keep improving, and you're going to be better off than when you started.

Step three, when you're feeling stuck and feel that you can't go any further, look at how far you've already come and remind yourself why you started.

You must be resilient intelligently, if the strategy you are pursuing isn't working change it, try something else that will work. Change your approach, not your goal.

> *"You don't have to see the whole staircase. Just take the first step."*
> – Martin Luther King

Self Discipline

Former President of the United States, Theodore Roosevelt, has a quote that just strikes me as so true, "With self-discipline, most anything is possible."

To understand discipline, you need to shift your mindset, from thinking that when you're disciplined that you're lacking or going without something. Being disciplined means that you are gaining something of greater value. Self-discipline is rather a set of behaviours bringing you closer to your goals.

Willpower, on the other hand, is a muscle and the more we use it, the stronger it gets. I have high confidence that you'll find the answers you're looking for through discipline. Military discipline trains you to follow orders, self-discipline, trains you to follow your goals and dreams.

One of my podcast guests shared with me a story that I was already familiar with, but when he said it, I knew I had to share it in my book.

They did a study at Stanford University, were a psychology professor took a group of 4-year-old kids and put each individual in a room by themselves.

They left each kid with a marshmallow and said, "When I come back in 15 minutes, and if you haven't eaten the marshmallow you can have another one, so then you will have two marshmallows."

When the professor returned, 2/3 of the kids had eaten the marshmallow. This one kid understood one of the keys to be successful. The ability to delay instant gratification. Let me blow your mind, they did a follow-up study 15 years later, where they discovered that the kids who didn't eat the marshmallows became the successful ones. They had gotten good grades in school, made it to university, and had good relationships with those around them. The kids who ate the marshmallow? Where not as successful and many hadn't made it to university. The moral of the story is, don't eat the marshmallow! If you are patient and don't settle, you can achieve all your goals. Here's how!

The CAT Method

Ladies and gentlemen, boys, are girls I present to you my very own unique acronym for goal setting called the CAT method. This model I developed is easy to remember and even easier to follow. Half of you probably procrastinate in work and watch videos of cats, so this should be relatively straightforward. CAT stands for Clarity, Actionable, and Tracking. Next is, The Time Frame element. This is the period of time for when you want to have your goal achieved. Allow me to illustrate by example, using a career goal on how to use the CAT time frame method.

Clarity - Let's imagine that currently, you are a trainee tax advisor with a goal of becoming a partner in the firm. Let's be real here. It is highly unlikely that this will happen overnight, that's why we need to get clear. I'll never forget strategy class in college when our lecturer said, "If you don't know where you're going, any road will take you there."

Most of us are clear on what we don't want versus the things we actually do want. Clarity comes when you surround yourself with people who are clear on what they want. This will rub off on you, but that's not all. Ask yourself if this is something that you truly want? If it is, ask yourself how you can make it even clearer?

Actionable - I've said it before, and I'll say it again, nothing gets done until you do the work. What are some of the actions you could take to get to being a partner of the firm? Well, I think if you followed the strategies that are in this book you would be doing a pretty good job. It's also an excellent idea to develop a plan of action. This is when you have a couple of small daily goals or rituals that if you can achieve every day will bring you closer to your goals. Let's say you complete 5 small goals a day; that's 35 small goals a week, and 1,825 small goals a year. That sure is a lot of goals. Small consistent actions lead to significant results. I love the quote, "Start small, think big and act now."

Tracking - You could also call this measuring your goal, I like to call it tracking so that you can keep track of the progress you are making. It makes sense that if you don't have a starting point achieving your goals is even more challenging because you get disoriented and lost along the way. Therefore, when you have a starting point, it's much easier to see how far you have come. Steve Jobs put it fantastically when he famously said when giving a speech to graduates of Stanford University, "You can only connect the dots looking backward."

Use a note pad or a journal so that you can monitor your progress. Writing in a journal is a common habit of the ultra successful, maybe you can do the same.

Time Frame - Probably the most important part of the whole goal setting process is the time frame. Set yourself a date as to when you want to have your goal achieved, as this date approaches you will be more likely to take action.

Chapter 3
How to Become a World Class Communicator

"The Single Biggest Problem in Communication, is the illusion that it has Taken Place." -George Bernard Shaw

In the 21st century, our communication mediums have changed. Now we WhatsApp, Facebook, or email rather than calling people, or visiting them in person. What hasn't changed when we communicate, is that most of the time another human being is on the other side. This chapter will not only open your mind as to how to communicate with diplomacy, but it will also show how messages of communication are interpreted.

In the workplace, communication is probably one of the most important factors. People need to receive clearly communicated messages, so they are on the right track and know what they are doing. It could be that you need to do some public speaking in the workplace, and your nerves are on edge worrying how to communicate your message. It's not only how we communicate with others that impacts our success. How we communicate with ourselves and overcoming internal negative dialogue is also the key to success.

Did you know that only 8% of our

communication is based on the words we say? Did you know that 37% of our communication is based on our tone of voice? Did you know that the remaining 55% comes from our facial expressions and body language? If you find this hard to believe, just think of when someone says something to you, and they come across as rude. A lot of the time, it was the way they said it, versus the actual words they said.

When communication is open, and employees are connected, research by McKinsey shows that productivity rises by 20% to 25% on average. What is even more staggering is that almost all communicators use too much jargon in their communication. Then they wonder why people misinterpret what they are trying to say. Only 6% of these communicators think creativity is being used to its full advantage when communicating clearly. Therefore, learning to communicate in clear and plain English will help you tremendously succeed in your career.

Public Speaking/Presentations

Did you know that people fear public speaking more than dying? One of the jobs I applied for, you had to do a presentation to board members as part of the recruitment process. I feel comfortable with presentations and public speaking, after all, I have been in front of audiences in the Unites States, Spain, and Ireland. So, I figured all this would stand to me, then one evening I had an inspiring thought. Just because I am a confident speaker, does not necessarily make me a good one.

I have seen people speak that are so boring I just wanted to go asleep. I have also seen many people speak that are boring but have great content. Then there are the people who are full of confidence when they're speaking and who are also full of something else. Then there are those that are full of confidence and who have great content, alongside a flawless delivery of their presentation.

I learned that this didn't come naturally for these people and that there was a method to their madness. People like Tony Robins are a great example or Barack Obama, those guys can speak. I decided that I would use my confidence as an advantage and that I would study how to communicate clearly and efficiently during public speaking presentations. This has served me well, and it's a skill I believe to be essential in today's workplace.

There's a group that helps people with their public speaking called Toastmasters. I have never been myself, but everything I've heard about Toastmasters has been positive. There's also a book called *The Quick & Easy Way to Effective Speaking* by Dale Carnegie. Moreover, I want to give you some tips I have found useful. A good presentation is well thought out and planned. When I was in college, I learned something about speaking that has stayed with me.

1. Tell the audience what you are going to tell them.
2. Tell it to them.
3. Then tell them what you've told them.

When you speak in this format, it keeps the listener engaged. I always try to get the audience excited so that they cannot wait to hear what you are going to say next. When delving a presentation, it's important to cut out technical jargon that your audience won't understand. To put things metaphorically, imagine that you're a rocket scientist, and you know all there is about how a rocket breaks through the atmosphere. Now, imagine trying to explain that to a seven-year-old child. How would you go about it? You must make it simple so they can understand. Perhaps you may illustrate things with examples or stories, like how I've done in this book. Conversing with your audience is also a simple technique that will make you an effective speaker. Nobody likes to feel intimidated, so make the audience feel like you are one of them. To get your point across be enthusiastic and put your heart into the presentation. Be yourself and express sincerity, credit those who are in the audience and thank them for listening to you. Spend time establishing yourself as credible to talk about what it is you're presenting.

I believe that your talk will only be successful if you can influence the audience. Ask the audience questions! For example, "Can I get a show of hands how many people here want to know the secret to success?" I call this audience participation. It's when you ask them to perform a particular action. This makes you more memorable as a presenter and yields greater results.

Open Your Mouth

Let's look at how communication can affect our lives when we don't use the correct medium. A man and his wife had been arguing all night, and as bedtime approached they weren't speaking to each other. It was not unusual for the pair to continue this war of silence for two or three days. However, on this occasion, the man was concerned. He needed to be awake at 4:30 am the next morning to catch an important flight, and being a very heavy sleeper he normally relied on his wife to wake him. Cleverly, he thought, while his wife was in the bathroom, he wrote a note on a piece of paper.

"Please wake me at 4:30 am, I have an important flight to catch."

He put the note on his wife's pillow, then turned over and went to sleep. The man awoke the next morning and looked at the clock. It was 8:00 am. Enraged that he'd missed his flight, he was about to go in search of his arrogant wife to give her a piece of his mind, when he spotted a hand-written note on his bedside cabinet.

The note said, "It's 4:30 am get up!"

Let's take this story as true for now. I'm not sure if it is or not. However, considering that 95% of divorces are because of the lack of communication between spouses, this story may be true after all. Whereas if the man had used oral communication with his wife and broke the silence, I feel he would've gotten a different response. How would you react if you faced a situation like that and relied on somebody to wake you? Let's look at how we could have addressed the situation to communicate better and get what we wanted in the first place. I think the best thing the man could have done was put aside their argument and his pride, then politely ask his wife could she wake him up. This would change the dynamic of the conversation and more than likely the man's response. Therefore, it's so important to use the correct medium of communication that works for you.

Build Rapport

When I was writing this chapter, I was experiencing writer's block. I kept asking myself what is the best way to communicate my point in a way everyone can relate to and understand. Suddenly I was in the shower, and it dawned on me. Be it leadership or communication it all comes down to influence. One of the best ways to communicate to someone is to establish the common interest, or what I call "Me Too" communication. You can also call this rapport building, or influencing them. We can build rapport through our words, as people will be able to relate to us if we use words like them. Have you ever been in a situation where you were talking to somebody, and you found out that you both support the same football team? Suddenly you were like, "I like this person." You might have equally been in the same situation where the guy supported a football team you did not like. Here you found yourself saying, "God damn United fans, wouldn't trust them as far as you throw them." It's funny how this affects our communication. When we don't like someone, we may withhold relevant information from this person. This is because our rapport is out of sync. This can be treacherous if you work with them. There's a way to solve it, and boy I'm glad there is. Otherwise, I'd be completely f@?*€d and have nothing more to write in this chapter.

I mentioned earlier that 55% of our communication is our physiology or our body language. That should be music to your ears as you can build rapport through body language. This is by matching and mirroring, for those of you who have no concept of what I mean, let me illustrate this for you through an example. Have you ever been talking to somebody and noticed how they crossed their arms a certain way? Or maybe how they sat in a relaxed position? Even things like the speed and tone of their voice?

These are all things we can copy to build rapport and better communicate with that person.

Imagine that it is 3:50 pm on Friday afternoon and you are a guy, and you kind of have a thing for one of your work colleagues. You notice that she is always well dressed and that she crosses her arms while standing. Also, she is always in a position of perfect posture when she is talking to people. She speaks with a soft tone of voice in a slow yet polite manner. Having plucked up the courage to ask her out on a date, and visualised the event in your head and her saying yes, you finally approach her. Little to your knowledge the pants you are wearing have a mud stain on them from when that car drove past you yesterday, your shirt is also sticking out on one side, and you haven't shaved in 3 days. So how can you influence this girl to go on a date with you? Well mirror her body language, speak the same language as her! While talking if she crosses her arms you subtly do the same thing, without making it obvious of course. If her tone of voice slows down or speeds up, match it.

Here's another tip that I find very useful. If you notice that throughout the conversation the person you are talking with doesn't use bad language, you shouldn't either. Rapport is only one part of communication. How the other person receives the messages is equally important.

Syntax

The next step is how we use language when communicating, or the syntax. I'm an affluent Spanish speaker and for those of you that speak another language will easily understand this. In Spanish they say, "Tengo Sed." If you were to translate that into English, it would literally mean, "I have thirst." You would never say that to somebody. You would simply say "I'm thirsty." The syntax is also important if you were to say, "Johnny bit the dog" versus, "The dog bit Johnny" same words but mean different things. Therefore, understanding the syntax is a crucial part of our communication.

If They Have a Name Use It

To borrow a concept from Dale Carnegie author of the legendary book *How to Win Friends and Influence People*. If you haven't already read it head over to my website and click on the "books to read" blog post and use the link there to purchase it. Dale talks about a simple, yet highly effective, and probably one of the most underused communication strategies out there. That is using the person's name!

We all love hearing our own name. Do you remember being a kid and walking into a store and seeing a stand with toy cars or trucks, on the stand with loads of different names? One of the first things we all did as children was look for our name, and we would be disappointed if it wasn't there. Why were we disappointed? I don't know. It's not like we were ever going to purchase the item. My point is that when we call someone by their name, it instantly makes the communication more favourable and personal. We like that as humans, we value when other people take the time not only to compliment us but when a person goes out of their way to make us feel important. So why not do the same in return, when we are trying to communicate and influence others.

See things from their Point of View
Often when we are communicating, we have our own interest at heart, and this is the total wrong way to go about it. Sometimes we are communicating with someone who loves to do all the talking, that is ok. The best way to communicate with them is to let them do the talking. Like charismatic leaders, communicators should also put themselves in the other person's shoes. It's important to know and understand what their desired outcome for your communication is, and do all you can to serve them.

Listen with Interest
I have said it many times before, two ears and one mouth for a reason. Not only will listening improve your communication skills, but it will also make you a better leader, more on this in the

next chapter. When listening, listen like you mean it, so that the other person feels heard. Listening is simply about being present in the moment. Highly effective communicators listen to understand, rather than blab to be heard. Listening is one of the main elements of the highly effective communicators. Make the other person feel understood. A good way of doing this is by rephrasing what you heard to ensure understanding. Acknowledge what they're saying with concern.

Remember Names
It's extremely friendly and personal when you meet someone for the second time, and they remember your name. Do you want to know what will have an even greater impact on your communication? What if you remembered their kid's names? What if you remembered the name of the school they went to, and the topic the studied? Try this the next time you meet someone for the first time, that you know you will meet again in the future. This sends them a couple of messages,

1. I like this person.
2. This person cares about me.
3. If needed I would help this person.

I don't know about you, but that's the kind of impact I want to have on others.

Ask Questions
For those of you that are Irish alarm bells be going off here as mammy told us, "Don't ask too many questions it's rude and nosey."
Well, Mammy may be right and wrong here. Correct in the sense that coming across as nosey is the last thing you want. Ask questions to your advantage, to demonstrate the following.

1. That you are interested in them.
2. Gather information to enhance the relationship.
3. It presents an opportunity for you to be a good listener.

Make an Impression
If you act on the strategies in this book, somebody somewhere is going to be saying, "Holy mackerel Johnny is going places." Why? This will because, "Johnny" (you) will now have the skills that the most successful people on the planet have. These skills are useless unless you make an impression on people. Here's how it's done. Like great leaders, you must learn to smile and communicate with your eyes and ears. Hold eye contact longer than is comfortable, touch them on their shoulder or arm if they are a touchy feely person. Sincerely compliment these people or else don't compliment them at all, and be open with your communication. Tell them something that you don't generally tell people, this builds trust and strengthens the relationship. If you want to understand what it takes to make a lasting

impression on people, go listen to my podcast with Gavin Duffy. The story about the plumber will inspire you and open your mind on how you can make an impression. For the information about accessing the podcast, check out the resources section.

I promise you that if you implement these strategies not only will you be a better communicator, you will be a connector, and when you connect your impact will change the world for the greater good.

Chapter 4
The Millennial Leader

"To Lead People Walk Behind Them." - Lao Tzu

Why Leadership is Important

Yesterday I was watching Tony Robbins as he live streamed his keynote speech at Dreamforce 2016. He was talking about as a leader, what are some of the specifics you can do to improve your level of engagement. This is something to think about because when you look at the statistics, they can be quite staggering. To become successful in your organisation leadership is going to play a huge role. Over a ten year period, companies who have strong leadership have seen a 900% increase in their stock price growth versus 74% in poorly led companies. What makes it even more unbelievable is that when a CEO is removed from their position, 73% of the time it comes down to bad leadership. So, if you want to make it to CEO what do you think you need to be good at doing? Leading! What's even more shocking is that 38% of employees are planning on finding a new job because of bad leadership in their organisation. I believe that this all links back to being under-appreciated at work, as the research suggests that 39% of workers do not feel appreciated. This is mind blowing when 77% of people admit they would work harder with a little bit of recognition.

The good news is that as a millennial, you have the open-mindedness to address this problem. That's why almost 50% of us millennials see ourselves being in a leadership role in the next ten years. Maybe even POTUS. Companies are starting to look at millennials as greater leaders than traditional leaders. If you look at Ernst and Young 59% of their senior managers are millennials. There are countless opportunities out there for millennials. However, some of us feel a sense of entitlement that the world owes us something for whatever reason that might be. Well, I'm here to tell you that the world doesn't owe you anything, and that leadership is much more about what we can give to the world, and not the other way around.

Leadership Starts Within

For those of you that would love an inspiring story that's hidden with lessons of leadership I recommend you pick up a book called *The Leader Who Had no Title* by Robin Sharma. You can find a link to purchase this book on my website. Setting that book aside for a moment, one of my core beliefs is that in the makeup of a world class leader lies a person who refuses to settle until their vision becomes a reality.

Let's take a couple of moments to appreciate leaders like Steve Jobs, Bill Gates and Mark Zuckerberg who have disrupted our generation regarding how we interact. Although the only

millennial here is Zuckerberg, we can relate to them all in our own ways. I'm not going to bore you with the story of Steve Jobs, as most of you already know he was the co-founder of Apple. He was kicked out of his own company to return many years later. What I find interesting about Jobs is his leadership philosophy. He had a core belief that Apple should be structured like the biggest start-up in the world. Why? Because start-ups are a haven for new ideas and innovation. I find it interesting that Jobs had a sense of urgency about him in the way he worked, and that this fuelled the things that needed to be done. Jobs was obsessed with beautiful design. He once quoted something along the lines that he wanted the icons on the first iPhone to be so beautiful that people would want to lick them. This design obsession was also for the interior of the products. When Jobs was a kid, he was once painting the fence. His father came along and said, "Good Job Steve, but what about the inside of the fence?"
Jobs replied, "Dad nobody will see the inside."
"I know, but we will." Said his father.

Upon completion of a project Jobs once asked his design guy to put his signature on the inside of the computer he designed.
His response was, "Steve nobody will see the inside?"
Jobs reply was one of excellence as he said, "I know but we will, and all artists must sign their work."

The leadership lesson I want to illustrate

here is that so often we are obsessed about what's happening in our outer world, that we forget to look at the real leader that's inside us. It's only when we search for that leadership inside of us, that the world rewards us as a remarkable leader. I'm far from a natural born leader, several years ago I would be clueless on to how to lead. Now having studied the topic, and put my knowledge into action I've learned that if I can become a leader we all can. You hold all the same qualities I have, but you just haven't opened yourself up yet to the endless possibilities being a leader will bring into your life.

Lead by Example

Do you want to know what real leadership is? Let me share with you a little story. The story goes that sometime close to a battlefield over 200 years ago, a man in civilian clothes rode past a small group of exhausted battle-weary soldiers digging an obviously important defensive position. The section leader, making no effort to help, was shouting orders, threatening punishment if the work was not completed within the hour.

"Why are you are not helping?" Asked a stranger going by on horseback.

"I am in charge. The men do as I tell them." Said the section leader, adding, "Help them yourself if you feel so strongly about it."

To the section leader's surprise, the stranger dismounted his horse and helped the men until

the job was finished. Before leaving the stranger congratulated the men for their work, and approached the puzzled section leader.
"You should notify top command next time your rank prevents you from supporting your men, and I will provide a more permanent solution." Said the stranger.

Up close, the section leader now recognised US President George Washington, (The guy on the US $1 bill for those who don't know him) and realised the lesson he'd just been taught.

I'm not sure if this story is true or just a made up old fable. Frankly, I don't mind. Doesn't it illustrate what real leadership is when you lead by example? Washington's key leadership ability was that he did not abuse his power. Fundamentally, leadership is more about empowering others, than it is about being powerful yourself.

John Adair, who wrote over 40 books in the area of leadership and management and is also known for his Action Centered Leadership approach. I believe Adair's elements complete a full circle that leads back to empowering others, as it combines getting the task done while developing the team and the individual.

Adair is also known for his 50:50 model, this means that 50% of motivation comes from the individual and the remaining 50% from the external environment. Something to ponder when you are feeling demotivated. Therefore, it may be an idea to get into the motivated environment. In my first book, I write about getting into the study environment, and how I only studied in the library as it contributed to my success. This is the same with leadership, Steve Jobs was known for creating, clutter-free environments to fuel creativity. You can model the success of these great leaders and learn from the experts.

Leaders Come Together

Another fable of real leadership is the story of The Boy in the Hotel. A man and a young teenage boy checked into a hotel and were shown to their room. The two receptionists noted the quiet manner of the guests and the pale appearance of the boy. Later the man and boy ate dinner in the hotel restaurant. The staff again noticed that the two guests were very quiet and that the boy seemed disinterested in his food. After eating, the boy went to his room, and the man went to reception and asked to see the manager. The receptionist initially asked if there was a problem with the service or the room, and offered to fix things, but the man said that there was no problem of the sort, and repeated his request. The manager was called and rapidly appeared. The man asked could they speak privately and was taken into the manager's office. The man explained that he was spending the night at the hotel with his fourteen-year-old son, who has been severely ill, probably terminally. The boy was soon to undergo therapy, which would cause him to lose his hair. They had come to the hotel to have a break together, and because the boy planned to shave his head that night, rather than feel that the illness was beating him. The father said that he would be shaving his own head too, in support of his son. He asked that staff be respectful when the two of them came to breakfast with their shaved heads. The manager assured the father that he would inform all staff and that they would behave appropriately.

The following morning the father and son entered the restaurant for breakfast. There they saw the four male restaurant staff attending to their duties, perfectly normally, and all with shaved heads.

This story follows Robin Sharma's philosophy of leading without a title. I believe that the lesson of leadership in the story is that when we go out of our way to help someone, we lead at a level that is authentic to ourselves.

Earlier today I was in my friend's Jacks house, we were discussing the progress with this book when I asked him, "What do you look for in a leader Jack?"
He said, "Encouragement, if they aren't encouraging they're not doing a very good job at leading."
Jack is right leaders need to be encouraging to have an impact. It's my belief that to lead, is to

serve others. To get people to do what you want, give them what they want. When we reach for targets that are higher than ourselves, our natural leadership abilities come to the surface. True leaders inspire and help others fulfil their potential in a growth orientated manner. *Leaders are humanitarians, who compliment when others criticize, accept while others judge, construct while others destruct, and they give when others take.*

To use a gardener as a metaphor, gardeners get the growing conditions ideal before they plant their seeds. When the seeds are planted the gardener nurtures the seeds by watering them and feeding the soil so that the seeds can grow! The result being that each seed turns into a healthy plant. That is exactly what leaders do, but instead of growing plants, they grow people. That being said, let's look at the skills you can adapt to become an even better leader.

LEADERS – Acronym

"Leaders don't make excuses, they create results." - Robin Sharma

Listen
God gave us two ears and one mouth for a reason. We should listen twice as much as we speak. Most people just want to be heard, that is why people pay expensive fees to therapists, so they can feel like they are heard. To listen effectively, look the other person in the eye and pay attention with an

open mind and do not interrupt them. So often *we listen to reply instead of listening to understand*. Taking the time to listen not only goes for the people in your organisation but the customers you serve and how to fulfil their needs.

I was at a conference when the value of listening really struck a chord with me. You know the movie The Secret? One of the stars of the movie is a lady called Lisa Nichols. Before the movie went into production, all the stars had gathered at a cocktail party type of event. Lisa felt uncomfortable to be in a room with such big stars, so she wanted to make the most of her time, and learn all that she could. She was talking to someone in particular, and they asked her a question, and she said something along the lines of, "Can you do all the talking? Because when I'm talking, you're not."

She wanted to learn, and she wanted to listen! I love the quote from the Dali Lama on this, *"When you talk, you are only repeating what you already know. But if you listen, you may learn something new."*

Empathise

Although empathy involves listening to understand, it takes it a step further. Empathising with someone must be done authentically, and it must come from a place where you are willing to put yourself into the other person's shoes. This is called cognitive empathy. I always empathise with people whenever I can. Everybody is fighting their own unique battle. Therefore, empathy goes a long way. Start caring more about people than anybody else does, when you care about others, they care about you. Feel what others are feeling, this is called emotional empathy. When you care about people, it's much easier to perform as a leader. As humans, we have the need to feel significant, and that our lives are important in the eyes of another. When we empathise, it makes others feel important. The only way to lead people and influence them is to let them know you have their backs. Show them empathy. It's not a sign of weakness; it's a sign of strength. A huge part of being empathic is knowing what others need from you. This is a strong quality in leaders and is called empathic concern.

Awareness
Leaders are aware of what is happening within their team or their organisation. I did a mock interview at a law firm in Dublin, where one of the paralegals had it set up to receive notifications if the firm was mentioned in the news. She knew what was going on in her organisation. Another technique to become more aware of what's happening is to ask questions to gather information, so that you can anticipate the road ahead. Reread the section on self-awareness. This is a quality of all world class leaders.

Decisive
Leaders need to be able to make decisions. Tony Robbins says that, "Change starts the moment we make the decision to change."

So much of leadership is about setting the direction going forward. For this to happen, some decisions must be made. This involves picturing yourself as a decisive person and eliminate worrying if you made the right decision or not. Real leaders go with their gut, and it's almost always accurate. Whatever is going good for you in your life right now, and whatever is going bad, it all started with a decision of some sort, so start making better decisions. To make good decisions as a leader, it's important to have good information. Sometimes we can be hesitant to make decisions without good information. When you get the information you need it's important to ask yourself, what happens if I make this decision now? Then ask yourself, what happens if I don't make this decision now? This will guide you to do the right thing.

Empower
I already mentioned that leaders empower others. The best way to truly do this is to be true to your values and the values of others. If you have a work colleague that wants to come to work an hour earlier, to leave an hour earlier, so they can make the gym before it gets busy in the evening. It's wise to let them do so, as they will work harder with you when you empower their values.

Before you understand others values, first understand your own. Give your team access to the best knowledge you can, the more they know, the more they will be able to do, and the more the can serve others. That's one of the reasons why I wrote this book so that I can empower millennials with the best knowledge out there.

I was listening to a podcast earlier about leadership, and I gained a valuable insight. Leaders should treat everyone like their mother. Imagine the impact you would have if you treated everyone with such integrity? I once came across a meme on Instagram that I posted on my page, and it sums up empowering people better than I ever could.

The Chief Financial Officer asks the CEO, "What if we develop our people and they leave us?"

The CEO responds by saying, "What happens if we don't and they stay?"

As a leader invest in your people and empower them.

Relationship Build

When you are in a position of power and leading, it's important to have stable relationships with those around you. You can't make it on your own all the time, so receiving help from others is part of what will make you a great leader. The key to stable relationships in the workplace comes back to what I have already said. Give more than you take, and always be looking for ways to add more value than everyone else. I once did a podcast with a guy where we talked about building relationships when he shared with me a golden nugget. Deposit before you withdraw. This is so true as you can't get money out of the bank if there's none there in the first place. The same is true with relationships. So, always, always, provide value first. Most of my successes to date have been down to my ability to build relationships with others.

Smile
The look on your face can say all it needs to say and can impact those around you in a negative or positive way. DO NOT HAVE A RESTING BLANK FACE! It's crazy to think that 69% of people find a woman more attractive wearing a smile, rather than makeup. A study by Wayne State University concluded that people who were smiling in their high school yearbook lived to an average of aged 80 while those who weren't smiling lived to an average of aged 73. So PLEASE smile, it won't kill you.

Chapter 5
Teamwork Makes the Dream Work

"Great things in business are never done by one person. They're done by a team of people." - Steve Jobs

We all Need to Belong

When you die, your funeral will be a result of teamwork. Four people will carry your casket to your resting place. My question is, if the dead can't RIP without teamwork, how can the living? In today's world, we all work as part of a team to get our job done.

We may be unaware of this, but if you take the train to work in the morning, it takes a team of people to make sure that train leaves and arrives on time. According to a report by ClearCompany, almost 50% of millennials cite they would give up a portion of their paycheck to have a more collaborative workplace implemented and to help increase productivity. To take things into a broader perspective, 39% of employees believe their organisation does not collaborate enough. On the other end of the spectrum, you've got 75% of employers, rating team working as very important. Yet as few as 18% of employers give their employees any feedback on the subject. Whereas, almost everyone (97%) of employees cite lack of collaboration as the main reason for projects being a failure in the workplace. It looks to me that today's workplace has a real problem with collaborating and working together as part of a team.

The need to belong is something we crave as millennials. We do not have to belong to the elite social group, but a social group that we feel comfortable around. Once we feel a sense of community from the workplace, we immediately want to engage more as a team. I think learning how to work in groups effectively is a vital part of our success moving forward in the future. Teamwork coupled with leadership and communication skills are the main components that will drive you into becoming the most successful millennial in your organisation.

Champions Do More

While researching for this chapter, I wanted to find some inspirational stories that would be relevant for everybody. This proved to be more complicated than I thought. So, I decided that I would use sports as an example.

Have you ever been watching your favourite sports team when suddenly they were facing defeat? Then out of nowhere, the ultimate comeback happens, and they go on to win the match? Well, why do you think that happens? It happens through teamwork.

Sports is not my forte, but I wanted to share

this example with you, just to illustrate just how powerful teamwork can be. I like to watch the Irish rugby team play, and they're an excellent example of how teamwork should look. If you are or are not a rugby fan, you will be aware that the All Blacks are world renowned for their team spirit, and their pre-match ritual called the Haka. Back in 2013 Ireland was achieving the impossible, just after 18 minutes of match time, Ireland had a lead on the All Blacks 19-0. This is unheard of, as the All Blacks were set to win all their international test games in that calendar year. Fast forward, and it was the 80th minute, and the All Blacks had caught up. Former Irish captain Paul O'Connell was confident he could hold them back and keep up the defensive effort going. This plan did not go as expected, as an All Blacks try was conceived. Hope was not yet lost as the All Blacks needed to score the conversion after the try to win the game. One of their players took the shot, and he missed, you would think that this would be a sigh of relief on Ireland's behalf, but you'd be wrong. Some of the Irish players failed to hold their nerve and prematurely ran toward the ball (as happens frequently). The referee blew his whistle, and the All Blacks had another opportunity at converting their try. Boom! They scored it, shattering Ireland's chances of a victory. Ireland may beat the All Blacks with a huge win one day, but not that day.

How did the All Blacks come back and beat

my beloved nation? We all know that the playing field involves more than grit, it takes real passion, love, courage, and your heart invested in the game to make a strong team work. One of the former All Blacks players held a unique mantra he would repeat when things were tough, "Champions do more." Not only does this just apply to the field, but it also applies in life. As it's the little things that make the big difference. Champions are willing to go a step further than the rest of us, in the gym, on the field, they are willing to work hard as a team. Truly believing in themselves that they have what it takes to become successful. Ireland is another excellent example of this, and our rugby team has overcome tremendous adversity, for a small island nation we've reached number 3 in the world's rugby rankings.

Stronger Together

As humans, we work better when collaborating versus competing. Until this trend catches on to the masses, we have a problem. In the corporate world, we are often put into teams competing against each other. I have come across lots of case studies online of this happening. The most common solution used by the teams that performed effectively was identifying the specific areas that needed attention. Then the teams came up with a customised plan to make it work.

Tech giant Google spent millions of dollars

and countless hours in researching what makes up the perfect team, and the results were mind blowing. There was absolutely no evidence to suggest that there was a way to form a perfect team. The good news for you is that even if you think you are not an active team player, you are contributing to the success of your team.

*"Coming together is a beginning, keeping together is progress,
working together is success."* - Henry Ford

Being a solopreneur is tough. I must motivate myself every day to get up and get the work done. Just the other day I was heading to a Motown music night with some of my cousin's friends when one of them handed me an envelope that said, "Food for thought." When I got home that night, I opened the envelope, to find the contents to be a cut out article from a magazine. When I read the article, I discovered it was the success story of David Novak, CEO of Yum. The parent company of brands like KFC, Taco Bell, and Pizza Hut. As I read on, I discovered how this guy became successful, and I also discovered his take on team building. First, he attributes that the challenging environment in which he grew up, helped him succeed when most people would've failed. Secondly, during his climb to the top, he learned that valuing and supporting your team, alongside recognising a job well done is one of the keys to a successful team. Wait, there's more, the guy is also a multiple bestselling author in the area of leadership. I plan on reading his latest book entitled *O Great One*. What better way to learn than straight from the horse's mouth?

How to Solve Conflict?

The legendary Steve Jobs once had a childhood experience that taught him an invaluable lesson. That is that arguments and debates, alongside disagreements, are completely necessary for good teamwork and collaboration. Why? Because they polish each other and they make good ideas great. Jobs was wise enough to realise that he was not the smartest man in the room and that he relied on other people's ideas.

Therefore, I believe that part of dealing with conflict is a matter of your own perspective, and realising that other people's ideas can be of value. Ever heard the saying, "There is more than one way to skin a cat."
When you find yourself with a challenged team member, and they just cannot see your point of view, try this. Get a piece of paper and write down the following two equations, 7+2=9, and 5+4=9.

Both calculations yield the same answer just took a different route.
Once you have this on paper, it's easy for them to see that there is an alternative. Now you can nicely say to the person, "I agree, you have most

definitely figured out another solution to our problem. I promise that your solution has been taken into consideration. First, let's try this solution."

Give the other person the benefit of the doubt, be sure to see their point of view and make them feel understood. Take responsibility for your own feelings, use the word "I" when making statements. If you go in saying, "You...." it automatically puts the other person in a defensive situation and will heighten the conflict even further. Avoid using the word "but" because when you say the word "but" in the height of conflict everything you said beforehand gets disregarded. Instead, use the word "and" I promise you'll notice the difference.

Teamwork is the same, and ideas don't work until you do. There's no real way of avoiding conflict, it will arise, but solving it will come down to the quality of attitude each individual team member has.

Lastly, do a self-evaluation, like it or not maybe you are the one causing the conflict. That's ok there's always one. Maybe you are sending the team the wrong message, and maybe the communication needs to be clearer. Control your opinion, and respond accordingly, teamwork is not the time to be hot headed. Be diplomatic and be composed when criticised. Ask yourself, what do I think? Why do I think this? Have I any evidence?

Delegation

Let's put our ego's aside for just a moment, as much as we think we can do things better than everyone else. We know that it's not necessarily true. I just read an e-mail from one of my favourite authors Robin Sharma. In this email, he speaks of the legendary Bruce Lee who had a commitment to mastery and always had the attitude of a beginner, so that he could learn more. Then Robin drops a nugget that put's it beautifully, "The moment you think you are amazing is the moment you lose the spirit that made you amazing to begin with."

You see I believe that true team collaboration is when you recognise the strengths of other team members and give them tasks you know they'll be great at doing. The work product of the team is incredibly powerful when ideas are implemented by people who have the skill set to do it better than you. To become a true team player, put yourself forward for tasks that you know you can inject your world class level information.

Decision Making

At the end of the day, us millennials can be an undeceive bunch of people. Half the time we cannot make up our minds on what we would like to have for breakfast, never mind decide on what is best for the team. Therefore, I believe that good teamwork is based on the right decisions being made. Moreover, great teamwork is a matter of those decisions being implemented by each member of the team. Decision making is important as it gets the ball rolling and puts the team to work. How can you make better decisions? Decision making is a resource, but it is also a muscle. How to we build muscles? You guessed it! Give them a workout. Your success in life will come down to the quality of your decisions. Such as, will you decide to look after your health in your youthful years to prevent sickness later in life. Will you party every weekend and spend all your money on alcohol? Or as Will Smith said, "People buy things they don't need, with money they don't have, to impress people they don't like."

    These are all decisions with different results. Like good leadership, good teamwork comes down to good decision making. You can't be right all the time, so learn from your mistakes. Einstein said it better than me, "The definition of insanity, is doing the same thing over and over and expecting different results."
So, change things up when they're not working.

Clear and Common Goal

Teamwork is about establishing common objectives and ensuring that everybody on the team is clear on what they must do to complete the task. Goal setting is important here, as two key activities play a role in the achievement of the common goal. The first one is accountability. Anytime I've been a team leader, holding members accountable has been one of my strong points. By nature, people are lazy and can procrastinate tasks they should do, if you fall into this category it's fine you are perfectly normal. When I was a team leader, I did things differently. I would follow up with everyone on my team just to check in with them and get a progress update on how far they have come along, and if they needed any help with the remainder of their tasks. The second part is instead of relying on resources, be resourceful. Ok, so what do I mean by this? This means that, when you think that you don't have the capabilities of getting things done, you will remember the mantra of the All Blacks rugby player, "Champions do more." The next step is to persist until you find the resources to get the job done. With this, I guarantee 99.9% of the time you will find the resources and be successful leading your team to victory.

How to Problem Solve

Those that focus on solving problems in their organisation, are usually the highest paid and fasted promoted. There's not a team in the world that doesn't face problems and challenges when working together. Often these problems limit us from getting the job done. When I was in college my friends and I regularly had to problem solve. We figured that if we learned how to do this effectively, it would not only benefit our education, it would help us succeed when we entered the workforce.

Problems are inevitable in the workplace, and when left unattended often become worse. I want to illustrate by example this problem-solving method that I use and has worked wonders for me, I learned it from Brain Tracy.

Let's say that you work in a tech firm, and your team is working to design and develop an app. So far things have been good, but right now you are faced with a problem. On the surface, the problem is you haven't got the work completed in time to present your work to senior management. What can you do? Well, follow the next seven steps to solve the problem.

1. *Define the problem.* So much time is wasted by people trying to solve the problem when they are not even clear on what is the problem. Gather all the facts, gather all the information from those

who are involved. In this case, I'm going to say that each team member wasn't fully committed to the project. They may have shown up to meetings late or didn't understand what their part in the team was. Now that we have the problem clearly defined we can move on to the next step.

2. *Ask what the possible causes are?* Well, people being late for meetings may be one cause. Their bus was late, or they had a doctor's apportionment are some examples. Maybe they didn't have the equipment they needed to perform their tasks. Whatever the reason this is an important step. Ask, how did this happen? Why did this happen? Be sure to log the possible causes. This will help prevent them arising again in the future. Find the route of the problem, use this as your starting point.

3. *What are all the possible solutions?* Let's think about this logically. Maybe meetings were put on at a bad time? Therefore, one of the solutions may be to hold meetings at times that are more convenient to each team member. Creating a list of all the solutions will solve 90% of problems in the workplace. A solution for getting people to show up for meetings on time may be holding them accountable if they don't turn up.

4. *Decide what solution you are going to choose.* Any solution is better than no solution. This way you are working towards solving the problem.

5. *Assign responsibility.* To get things done, each person must know their role in solving the problem. Who's going to do what? When will they do it? What standard are they going to do it too? Setting a baseline is important. In this example, a standard to set may be that everyone is on time for scheduled meetings.

6. *Measure the results of solutions.* My college buddies reading this will be thinking, "If you're not measuring, you're not managing."
Something that was drilled into us all during our final year. It makes perfect sense to be measuring your progress. Problem-solving needs to have deadlines, so you can move on from a solution that isn't working.

7. *Task yourself.* The more you focus on solutions, the better you become at solving problems. Nominate yourself to put some of the solutions into action.

How to Get Full Commitment from Team Members

Teams work like clockwork when everyone is fully committed of course. There are several stages a team will go through when coming together. They are forming, norming, storming, and performing. At the forming stage, this is the best place to receive the full commitment from everybody. The key to commitment is when there's an invested emotional interest in the result the team is striving to achieve. This can be achieved by triggering their why. Let them know why the outcome of this project is important to them. Next, the forming stage, helps with recognising weak links, they are on every team, and it also presents an opportunity to nip that one in the bud. Then, the forming stage of the team, and for maximum results, conduct the following exercise. It can be performed by the leader, or if you are not the leader, please have the confidence to complete this exercise. This exercise works on the psychological principle of social accountability. Here's how it works, go to each member of the team and have them repeat the following sentence in front of everyone.

"Hi my name is '_____, ' and I am fully committed to working as a team player in accomplishing our tasks by doing whatever it takes for the team and by the team."

The reason why this is so powerful is that we don't like to fail in front of others, especially not after we say it out loud in front of people we see on a frequent basis. The final stage is performing. This is where everyone on the team comes together at gets to work to achieve their goals.

Chapter 6
What Time is it?

"A man who dares to waste one hour of time has not discovered the value of life."
-Charles Darwin

The Importance of Time

I'd like to start this chapter by sharing a note I found on the internet from an unknown source, that will help you realise the value of time.

To realise the value of One Year! Ask a student who has failed his exam. To realise the value of One Month! Ask a mother who has given birth to a premature baby. To realise the value of One Week! Ask an editor of a weekly newspaper. To realise the value of One Day! Ask a daily wage labourer. To realise the value of One Hour! Ask the lovers who are waiting to meet. To realise the value of One Minute! Ask a person who has missed the train, bus, or plane. To realise the value of One Second! Ask a person who has survived an accident. To realise the value of One Milli-Second! Ask the person who has won a silver medal in the Olympics.

You've Got Time

Ever wish like you had more time to do the things you loved? Time management can be a boring subject, so I promise I'll keep it as interesting as I can. You could define time management as the ability to plan and control time effectively to achieve our goals. We've all heard the phrase, "If you want something done, give it to a busy person."

This can be hard to wrap our heads around sometimes, as during the working day, the average person is interrupted every 8 minutes. Amazingly the average interruption lasts for 5 minutes. This can typically lead up to 50% of the time during our working day spend on distractions. Let's call a spade a spade, that's a lot of unnecessary time at the water cooler. With these figures in mind it makes me wonder, how does anybody get anything done? Then again I was a student, and we can do amazing things in short periods of time. What is even more staggering is that 80% of these interruptions are of little to no value and are avoidable. We've all been there and been distracted when we should've been working.

While motivation is a wonderful attribute to get things done, I came across a study that concluded that it wasn't motivation that made the difference in our engagement with tasks at work. Moreover, what makes the difference is when we learn productivity and time management skills. In this chapter, I want to give you the best strategy to effectively manage your time. So that you will have more time for, friends, family, and all the things that make your life that little bit better. Leveraging your time will fast track you to success in the workplace and help you achieve your personal goals!

The 3 Dimensions

We've all been in the position in our personal lives when it seemed like there weren't enough hours in the day to get everything on our to-do list completed. However, somehow we managed to get it all completed. It all just seemed to fit in.

There's a story of a university professor delivering a presentation on time management. You may have heard this story before as it has gone viral. I'm sure if you Google it you will find it.

The story goes that the professor was using visual aids to get his points across. He had a bag of sand, a bag of pebbles, a bag of rocks, and an empty bucket. He then asked for a volunteer in the class to fit all the items into the empty bucket. Naturally, one of his students volunteered and proceeded to put the sand in the bucket first, then the pebbles, and then when he got to the rocks they all wouldn't fit. The professor was using this as an analogy for poor time management. Each of the items represented something different. The rocks represent the important things we must do. Like making time for our family and having good relationships with those around us. The pebbles were also important things but did not require our immediate attention. These are things like exercise and building a fulfilling career. The sand was a representation of the inessentials that take up the bulk of our time. Things like social media that so many of us put before spending time with loved ones or doing exercise. Or things like being angry at those we care about most. Life is too short not to pay attention to the important things.

The professor then proceeded to fill the bucket with the rocks, then the pebbles, then the sand, as he concluded with the moral of the story. Make time for the important things!

Don't Be Fooled

This reminds me of the story of the executive who was on vacation on one of the Caribbean islands in a fishing village, where they live a relaxed lifestyle. He came across one of the local fishermen and complimented him on his fine catch. The executive was curious as to how long it took the man to acquire such a fine catch.

The man replied, "Oh it took me maybe two hours."

To which the executive replied, "Oh and what do you do with the rest of your time?"

The man kindly responded, by saying he sleeps in late, he takes a nap in the afternoon with his wife (Kinky Oldman) and spends time with his children.

"Why don't you stay out longer and catch more fish and make more money?" was the reply of the executive.

The man replied, "To what would I do with the extra money?".

"Well," said the executive, "You could invest in boats, and have some people working for you to make you, even more, money."

The old man said, "I don't really have much of a business knowledge."

The executive replied, "I've got a Harvard MBA, I can give you all the business advice you need."

The old man said, "Well I don't know, this sure sounds like it would take up a lot of my time."

"About ten years." the executive said confidently.

The old man was inquisitive and asked, "Then what will I do?"

The executive proceeded to say, "Well then you can retire in a small fishing village and sleep late and take naps with your wife and have time to play with your kids."

The moral of the story is that this is already what the old man was doing with his time. This story is much longer as I'm sure you are aware, but the point I want to illustrate is: Be careful what you spend your time doing, as sometimes it can be a long road to where you already are right now.

Lessons in Time

I had taken a one year course before I started college in Ireland, I took the course pretty seriously, but I recall one moment in particular.

Our course coordinator was a woman named Mary, one day Mary said to me that the ones who didn't take this course seriously, will not understand the value of that year, or their time until they look back many years in the future.

This just made so much sense to me and I could relate to it on so many different levels. The first one being that, all we really have is our time. We can make money, time and time again, but the one thing we cannot get back is our time. The second level I could relate to this on is that as humans we overestimate what we can do in a year, but underestimate what we can do in ten years.

Every single day we wake up with 86,400 seconds, and every day we have the same 24 hours as Beyoncé and Mark Zuckerberg. How we spend that time is entirely up to us. Focus on using your time for growth activities. Keep this phrase in mind "The days are long, but the years are short" now I can't cite the source other than my cousin Declan. However, it is one powerful line. Are you ready for the best strategies for effective time management?

Learning to Say No

Everything that I've learned about time management and drawing from my personal experience, learning to Say No crops up every single time. What this means is saying no to things that are not going to bring value, either to your work or to your life. Focusing on your one big thing is 100 times more important than focusing on 100 little things. What this means is that you should say no, to more opportunities than you should, say yes. Only say yes to opportunities that will contribute to your goals, not take from them.

To do Lists and Scheduling

Did you know that by spending 1hr planning you can eliminate up to 10hrs of work? We've all heard the phrase "failing to plan in planning to fail", but that really can be the case when it comes to our working lives. Being organised with a structured routine is a common trend among effective time managers. That being said, learning to schedule properly can be really effective and a valuable skill to obtain. Employers will value this greatly.

These days we've moved on from writing in our diaries, and we can now electronically schedule, with tools such as Google Calendar and Outlook Calendar. The key here is to block of time periods in your schedule for the important tasks. Approach these tasks with a high level of importance and with a sense of urgency, to make sure they get done.

A powerful technique is to plan your day the night before and plan your week on a Sunday evening. One tool I like comes from Robin Sharma, who makes a point to have a distraction free 90 minute work period at the beginning of your day. During this period your focus is on the important things. So, turn off your mobile phone and get things done.

I recently had the pleasure to see Robin speak in Dublin. He shared a tactic to increase focus, that is turning off our notifications for our emails. When we get a notification, and we check it, the brain gets a kick of dopamine, and we get hooked on notifications. The next morning, I had breakfast with a guy who tried this tactic, and he reported it to be a game changer! There's software called Cold Turkey that will block you from entering social media during your work period. I highly recommend you install it if you are someone who will find it difficult to stay away from social media.

Speed Reading

I wrote about this topic in my first book. Here I'm just going to explain the benefits to you. The average reading speed is approximately 200 words per minute. The average working person reads 2 hours per day. Taking a Speed Reading course will help you improve the reading rate to 400 words per minute, this will on average save you an hour per day. What could you do with that extra hour in your day? Check out, Tony Buzan. He's the master of speed reading.

The Pareto Principle

There once was an Italian economist called Pareto, he was the founder of the 80/20 rule. He basically concluded that 20% of our actions were responsible for 80% of our results. Imagine how successful you would be by focusing on that 20% all the time? It is much easier said than done but is entirely possible. The key here is to concentrate on the results generating elements of your to-do list. What's the best way to find out what items produce the most results? Ask yourself, if this task was complete what would the outcome be? From there it becomes a process of elimination.

The Power Meeting

I don't know about you, but I find it astonishing that 90% of people daydream during meetings, and 60% of people that take notes, just do so to appear that they are interested. A lot of the issues that are brought up during meetings, really are of little significance. A key tip is to have meetings that are aspirational. You may ask what do I mean by this? What I mean here is to have a meeting that leads to a particular set of actions that will ultimately get things done. Think about how much more productive you can be with a POA? (plan of action).

I was listening to the Gary Vaynerchuk audio book *Crush It*. Gary said when he was pitching to potential clients he'd schedule a meeting for one hour. He knew during the first twenty minutes of the meeting if the prospects would become a client. When he got the feeling that they wouldn't, he would end the meeting and spend the remaining forty minutes setting up more meetings with more potential clients. Now some of Gary's meetings are as little as four minutes.

Productive Period

The average worker gets around 6hrs and 57mins of sleep a night. Then when they rise they're dependent on coffee to kick start their day. It's really important to get enough rest as it can hold us back from performing to our potential. Recently I was listening to the Tim Ferris show, where Arnold Schwarzenegger gave his tips on how to get a good night's sleep. He said up to 2 hours before bed he stops using his mobile phone and stays out of debates on social media.

The light on the screen of our smartphones trick us into thinking it's daytime and the brain finds it hard to shut down. Remember that rest is the key to productivity, you cannot perform on an empty tank. We all have a time that we are highly alert and productive. For some of us it's the first thing in the morning and others it's late at night. The key is to find that period of productivity and do your best work then.

Delegation

Earlier today I was on the train on my way home reading Richard Branson's book *Finding My Virginity*, one of the lines on the page was, "My secret to success in business over the last fifty years." You guessed it delegation. You do not have to do everything! I repeat you do NOT have to do everything. Analyse your activities and figure out what you do best. Then figure out what you do poorly, and delegate that task to somebody who can do it better than you. Not only will this free up some of your time, but it also creates a work product of a much higher quality. Richard become an expert in building teams that worked together, it's no surprise the Virgin group is worth five billion dollars.

Chapter 7
How to Stay Engaged at Work

"Be humble, be hungry and always be the hardest worker in the room."
- Dwayne 'The Rock' Johnson

Do you find your work engaging? If yes, then why? If no, then why not? I'm going to take a complete guess right here and say that you don't. The research shows that 88% of employees have no passion for their work. Up to 80% of senior managers are also reporting they've no passion. Would you believe that this level of disengagement costs the US economy $500 billion per year? To top it all off, we constantly face interruptions and distractions in the workplace. Social media accounts for 57% of these distractions. It is almost like when we are working we care more about what is going on in other people's lives, than our own. These figures are staggering! So, after we get distracted, how long do you think it takes to refocus? On average, it takes about 25minutes to refocus on our tasks. Can you start to see how this might be a problem?

I don't know about you, but there's one thing for certain about me, and that's I believe that work should be something you are passionate about doing. Something that every morning when you wake up, you can't wait to get to work. Instead, most people fall into the trap of Monday morning blues and the "I can't wait until Friday" mentality. Then they wonder why their work life is a mess. Mainly because they do nothing to improve their situation. In this chapter, I want to share with you the tools and strategies you can use to make your work more engaging. In a way that they can be applied from today, and in a manner that's relatable.

Let it Flow

Have you ever wondered how people perform at their absolute best? I know that you want to learn their secret. I hate to break it to you but there's no secret to high performance, in fact, it's relatively straightforward. Mindfulness is one of the buzz words these days, it's also one of the keys to unlocking your peak performance. We will discuss how you can become more mindful later in the book.

However, according to a study, 83% of American workers are disengaged from their work. The reaming engaged workers are accessing a state of flow. What is flow? Flow is an altered state of conscious that is accessed when our brain is focused on certain triggers, that by evolution our brain has been trained to focus on.

Sounds a bit crazy, doesn't it? However, it makes sense. I first learned about flow when Steven Kotler was on my podcast. He says that one of the triggers for getting into this state of flow is a risk. Our brain pays more attention to those things that have consequences. We're always more engaged when we're faced with some risk. Have you ever procrastinated something? I mean right up until the deadline, and were super focused on getting the task completed? Of course, and you were super focused because unknowingly you were working in a state of flow. Being innovative and thinking outside of the box also helps us access a state of flow.

My favourite part of the podcasts is the conversation at the end when we are no longer recording. I just have to share what Steve shared with me, that is, we have learned all we need to know about high performance by the time we're finished kindergarten. It's really simple, take naps when you're tired, eat when you're hungry, and always be curious.

You Should Do It

My best friend Jack is an exceptionally good secondary school teacher in Ireland. One of the problems he faced when he started teaching was keeping his students engaged. I'm sure we've all being there sitting in class and not really paying attention to what the teacher is saying. I know this because I was once that student.

A few months back I returned to my old school to give a presentation on my first book, and to inspire the kids to go on to college, and how they can be successful in college. During my talk, I faced the same challenge as Jack, on keeping the students engaged. One day over coffee, Jack and myself were discussing how he keeps his students engaged. This is where he shared with me his very unique, but ingenious technique. When it comes to giving his class homework, he takes a different approach. If the class is well behaved, they are given an opportunity to start their homework, 10 minutes before the class is over. Then they've three options set out by Jack for when they get home.

1. A Must Do Task.
2. A Can Do Task.
3. A Should Do Task.

The "Must Do Task" is the bare minimum the student must do so that they can avoid punishment (Like some of us at work). The "Can and Should Do Tasks" are what gives the student extra room for growth. They feel very rewarded within themselves. What's interesting about his technique, is that his students almost always have their homework completed. Even the students who are "Class Clowns" are engaging with their homework.

For those of you who read my first book, you will be aware that I have a learning difficulty in written expression (Ironic for an author I know). Every presentation I've done, I've noticed a pattern in the room. The ones that are at the front are usually highly engaged and listen attentively.

The ones in the middle are usually listening, but are not quite sure as to what's happening. Then there are the ones at the back, who are either looking to avoid participation in exercises or do not care about what's happening. They are more interested in what's happening on social media.

This all changed for me one day. I was giving a presentation to young kids in a school, who had absolutely no interest in learning about the strategies I teach for success in college. These kids were laughing, joking, and thought that this was just going to be another one of those boring talks they were forced to attend, but will tag along because it gets them out of class. About one-quarter of the way through the talk I knew I needed to change the dynamic in the room. Randomly, I started to share my story of how I overcame the many challenges I faced in school, and I explained how I got to where I am today. What staggered me is that they all started to listen attentively and that my story really engaged them. I had everybody's attention, and you could hear a pin drop in the room. I didn't think much of it until later that day, when I received a text message from one of the students' parents. They said, how their child was inspired by my presentation that day, and to keep up the good work as I may have changed the direction in some of those kids lives. My talk may have inspired them, but getting that text and hearing that I potentially made a difference in their lives, that is what inspires me.

You may be thinking; how does that relate to workplace engagement? Think of it this way. If you start by taking a little more interest, in what you can do, instead of just doing what you must do, your work life will change. I promise, not only will this increase your engagement, but it will help you find purpose in your work. Which I know will lead to a more fulfilling life.

Find the Passion

Having said that, what do you think some of the rules of engaging with work are? And how can they be applied? Well, we know what disengages us, and that is a lack of passion. I believe passion can be discovered, even in things that we might not be passionate about doing. For example, have you ever been at a football game for two teams that you didn't support? But the passion of the winning team rubbed off on you. Suddenly you were passionate about that team in a way like never before.

Moreover, I'm a firm believer that you need to be passionate about your job, or else it's work, and not your life's fulfilling purpose. However, sometimes we need to do things we are not passionate about, to reach the things that we are passionate about doing. For example, I'm not passionate about posting on social media, but I know that it's something I must do, to grow my profile. So, when I deliver presentations, my audience can get to see them or to get people to listen to my podcast. Which is something I'm passionate about and making it happen. Often we are unaware that by taking a job that we don't want, how it can be the key to accessing the job we do want. The hardest part of getting our dream job, in a dream organisation, is getting our foot in the door. Everyone always puts their best foot forward, to really stand out, keep bettering the foot. Once you're in, it becomes up to you, to put your brand out there. You many consider starting as an intern, work your way up from there. Look for ways you can engage with the work (perform the should do tasks).

Surround yourself with people in the workplace who are extremely passionate about what they do, and I guarantee it will rub off on you. Senior management will then notice that this is what you are truly passionate about, and you will find yourself in a new role. Many organisations will offer job rotation, some of the jobs you will love, others not so much. That is fine, just be passionate about everything you do, and I promise opportunities will be presented to you that will not be presented to others. Many CEO's started out by doing jobs for the company they did not want to. They had the bigger picture in mind. If it works for them, I know that it will work for you.

Passion = the key of engagement. Keep searching until you find your passion, you may need to change course, you may need to go through a tough time to get there, but when you do, I promise it's worth the work. Ask yourself this question, is this my true passion? Never settle!

How to Beat Procrastination
Quick question, did you make your bed this morning? Yes? Good, you're well on track to beating procrastination. No? Well if you can't make your own bed, how are you going to tackle the bigger things you've been procrastinating? It's funny how we never procrastinate things we actually like doing. Search for meaning in the tasks you're putting off, like we discussed, find the passion. When we don't perform the tasks we've been resisting we give them power. However, when we perform those tasks, we take the power back. Not only does this strengthen your willpower, but it also rewires your brain. The crazy thing about procrastination is that we usually must perform the task we're resisting anyway. So why not get it out of the way? Research says that this can cause all sorts of stress and can even be linked to heart disease.

I once heard a great nugget from a book I've read. Something along the lines of if it can be done today, it should be done today. I always remind myself of that when I find myself procrastinating. Picture the task as already complete and see yourself having reaped the benefits of performing such a task. Reward yourself when you make some progress. If you feel anxious about starting something, accept that feeling, don't try to fight it, use it to empower you.

How to Stay Focused

There's a story I've heard about Warren Buffett, Bill Gates, and Gates's father at a dinner party. A guest asked them what the most important quality was for success today and all three responded "Focus" at the same exact time. These guys are the real experts.

One of the keys to staying focused is to stop multitasking, it negativity impacts our brains and attention span. It's also a good idea to train your brain, and there are tons of smartphone apps for this that you can use during your commute time. This may sound crazy, but if you need to refocus stare into space for a few moments. This works well when you work in front of a computer. Use the 20 - 20 - 20 rule, every 20 minutes stare at an object 20 feet away for 20 seconds.

Show Initiative

Take on side projects in the workplace and seek opportunities where you can express your passion. Employers love when you show initiative. You don't always have to succeed on those tasks, you make yourself valuable when you show initiative. Those who bring value to organisations are the ones who receive the big rewards! If you are working with customers on a frequent basis, take an interest in what they say. In doing so, you have more of a reason to be engaged.

Utilise your Network
If you are feeling disengaged or maybe stuck on a task, and you have no idea how to overcome it? Have you ever considered someone outside of your organisation? But in the same industry that can help you. This is where building networking partners can help you stay engaged as you feel a sense of support, and that you are not the only person in this situation. This can be a huge help overcoming that obstacle. This will also keep you engaged as you feel held accountable by those in your network.

Improve your Environment
We all know that Google and Apple are among the top companies on the planet with the best working conditions. Google is popular for having all sorts of luxuries at work such as bean bags, free food, gym facilities, and child care services. These amenities help keep employees engaged, as they work in an environment that encourages them to be creative.

Unfortunately, not everyone has the luxury of working for such a company. However, there are some things you can do to be more engaged as an employee. Invest in a comfortable chair so that your posture is in line, and you also prevent future back problems. I know that some companies allow you to bring pets to work, this may not be a deal breaker, but some people like to be around their pets. Stay away from negativity and gossip, avoid distractions at all cost. This is a game changer.

Recharge
You may be burned out and need to recharge the batteries. When you are burned out, it can lead to all sorts of problems such as stress, and it can also disengage you from the task you are focusing on. The best way I know to recharge the batteries is to make sure that you are hydrated, and are getting enough sleep, and living a healthy lifestyle, while simultaneously taking time for solitude and mindfulness. Remember how you learned about this in kindergarten? Take a nap.

Minimise Your Distractions
As mentioned above we are distracted so much from our work it's easy to wonder how anything gets done. Most distractions can be easily avoided. The key here is to find the source of the distraction and then eliminate the distraction. Better time management (As outlined in this book) will help you avoid distractions. When I find myself distracted, I'm human it happens all the time. I ask myself a magic question to get my head back into the game. Will this distraction take me closer to my goal? If the answer is no, it's back to work. I remind myself of the importance of my work and my goals to help people, the effect this has on me is amazing. I've found my passion, staying engaged is easy.

How to Perform at Your Peak

Let us take a moment to address a small, but crucial, part of peak performance that is often overlooked. We touch on this in the team working chapter. That is decision making. A lot of peak performance is about making the right decision at the right time. President Obama said that you will only ever see him wear blue or grey suits. He said it's because he has enough important decisions to make without worrying about what he's going to wear or eat.

In the book *Your Brain at Work* by David Rock, he writes that our ability to make decisions is a limited resource. Peak performers don't waste their energy on minor decisions. This means we need to be monitoring our focus and where our energy goes. Remember that where focus goes, energy flows. Therefore, it's important to ensure we focus on the result producing activities. This is to enable us to perform at our peaks. It's not just President Obama. Many successful people wear the same clothes or have a "Signature Look." Take Steve Jobs and his turtlenecks for example.

I recommend that you head to my friend JP's website and get a free copy of his book *The Peak Performance Principles*. I saw Jack Canfield speak at the Pendulum Summit in Dublin, where he held up JP's book and said, "This is a really good book, everyone should read this." So, if it's good enough for Jack Canfield, it's good enough for you.

Eat Less and Move More
I once read in an article, that fitness was the key to success in business. This also applies to the workplace. I think it's wise to get eating the proper foods. Also, this will not only prolong your life, but it will also give you more energy. If you listen to the podcast, I did with my friend Donald Carlson. You will know that he lost 38 pounds in 3 short months. He did this by starting to work out and eating the correct foods. Now he has so much more energy, and he's even getting up earlier and working harder on his business.

Move Forward Not Backward
Those who are performing at their peak understand one simple principle. That is that when you learn something new and apply it, magic happens. Like great leaders, peak performers love to learn and study. When you know more, you can do more. The ones who are highly engaged at work, are the ones that go to conferences. They are the ones reading the books, listening to the podcasts, consuming all they can to better themselves. Instead of putting their notes away, never to be seen again, they immediately take the actions that will bring them closer to their goals. When it comes to engaging with work, more often than not, it's easier said than done. *If there is one thing I have learned, and that is, sometimes we must act our way into feeling, more than we can feel our way into acting.* What this means is that when we are not feeling like

engaging with work, that is the moment when we need to do so the most!

Chapter 8
How to Rise to the Top

*"You will never reach your destination if you stop and throw stones at
every dog that barks."* - Winston Churchill

By now you should be thinking and planning for your success. I know, and I truly believe that you can do it. However, it's up to you to implement everything I've shared with you. I know that right now you've got your goals committed to paper and will do whatever it takes to follow through. As millennials chasing success, we will be faced with competition, but we are much stronger together. Trust me, the person who is a real team player, and wants the help others to succeed, are the ones who become the most successful.

A little self-promotion is healthy, but appreciation is what will take you to where you need to go. The rise to the top is a journey, and you will inevitably lose focus and motivation along the way. How will you overcome these hurdles? The best way that I know is to celebrate and reward yourself for the small wins. Don't wait until your CEO to call yourself a success, celebrate when you are recognised for doing good work. You need to be careful though. There is a quote that I hold as a strong value of mine that is "Nothing fails like success." What this means is the moment you become successful is the moment you stop doing the things that made you successful.

On a side note unless being on your phone is part of your job, block yourself from using social media for personal use inside the hours of work. This is extremely unprofessional and will damage your chances of success. What do you think is the biggest sin on social media? The biggest social media mistake that you can make is complaining about your job online. Be proactive on your social media, build your personal brand and promote your organisation as a wonderful place to work. Unless your contract prohibits you from posting about the organisation. Do you want to dive into my quick and actionable tips for your success? Vamos!

Taking to the Skies
Becoming an airline pilot is no easy task, the costs are substantial, in the region of €100,000 I believe. I read an inspiring success story in one of Irelands leading newspapers, about a woman that grew up dreaming of becoming a pilot. She didn't have access to this kind of money, but it was her dream. She decided to set herself a goal to become a pilot by age 30.

By the time she had finished college she had saved €20,000 and was hoping that it would be enough to secure a bank loan for the €100,000 that she needed. It wasn't, and she was refused. Determined to achieve her goal she returned to the bank the following year with €30,000 and the answer was still no.

Then for the first time in ten years, one of the airlines opened their cadetship programme. She applied and was sent ten aptitude tests to complete online. Two weeks later, she received an email to say that her application had been unsuccessful. She was heartbroken but determined to succeed, she drove to the nearest bookstore and purchased five books on taking aptitude tests. She took one every day while waiting for the cadetship to reopen so she could reapply.

To increase her savings, she decided to become a personal trainer to make some extra money. She then discovered a niche in the market for cupcakes. So, she flew to London and took a one day course in cupcake making. This was the start of her cupcake business. Originally selling to friends and family, the business exploded, she managed to sell 10,000 cupcakes in one year.

Booking a ticket to the US, she decided to get her private pilot's licence. One month later the airline reopened their cadetship programme. This time she passed the aptitude tests and was invited to a group interview. A few weeks passed, and she hadn't heard anything back from the airline, so she continued her private pilot training. After 10 hours with an instructor, she was sent on her first solo flight. On her second solo flight, shortly after take off and 800ft in the air, her engine failed. This greatly knocked her confidence, none the less six weeks later she returned to Ireland with her private pilot's licence.

One month later she got a call from the airline to say she made it to the next stage of the interview process. She tried not to get her hopes up, there were only 18 spots, and 3000 people had applied. The interview went well, so she was sent for a mental and physical evaluation. Then one evening while driving home she got a call from the airline to say, "Welcome to the team." She did it! She was resilient.

Her family and friends lined the runway for her first landing in Dublin, just two weeks before her 31st birthday. She had reached her goal by the skin of her teeth.

When you are willing to do, whatever it takes, you will overcome the challenges along the way.

How to Have More Confidence

To put it bluntly, the quickest way to get more confidence is to get around confident people. You need to be careful though because there's a fine line between cockiness and confidence. Cocky people think they know everything and that they are God's gift. Donald Trump is a cocky guy. A confident guy is someone like Gary Vee who knows his strengths and constantly improves them. Another great way to get more confidence is by doing whatever makes you feel confident. For example, if you need more confidence to talk to girls/boys whoever, by just going and doing it once will give you all the confidence you need to continue. Nike got it right, "Just do it."

Early to Bed Early to Rise
It is very common for successful people, like CEO's, to have started their day well before 6 am. I'm not a doctor, but one thing I know that will help you on your journey to the top is getting enough sleep. Without it our bodies begin to shut down, it's during our rest periods that our body repairs itself. I try to get 8 hours; it works for me, some people need more. Just be cautious not to underestimate the power of sleep.

One of my friends is among the highest paid coaches in the UK. He said it best, "Rest fuels high performance." Count your blessings before your sleep and pass your problems to a higher power. When rising give yourself 10 minutes to feel and express gratitude, meditate, or exercise. These 10 minutes will be the most empowering 10 minutes of your day and sets you up to succeed.

Arrive 45 Minutes Early, Leave 15 Minutes Late
When Jesé Rodríguez signed for Real Madrid he wanted to impress his coaches, so he decided to show up for training 2 hours early. To his surprise, Cristiano Ronaldo was already there training. Do you think this explains why Ronaldo is one of the highest ranked footballers in the world? I'm a big believer that so much of success comes from just showing up. Once you are showing up, I guarantee you are on the right path.

Avoid Negativity
As we become the sum of the five people we spend most of our time with; it's important that these five people uplift us. Please make sure that these people are positive, and will encourage your success, no matter how crazy your dreams seem. Stay away from the naysayers, these people are the toxic energy vampires that will crush you.

If you feel like you need an uplift visit my Instagram @thehabitsofsuccess for some inspiration. In your free time, of course. Always remember that it's the negative people who have the problem, not you. Let things go, and swiftly, shift your focus to the next value adding growth activity.

Improve Yourself
What if every day you got 1% better? Over the course of a year, you would improve by 365%. That is a massive improvement in such a relatively short period. The best way I know how to do this is by growing. Grow every day by stretching your limits. If you can do ten push ups the only way to get to 20 is start at 11, then push yourself to 12,13,15, etc. Eventually, with enough consistency you will reach 20, that is how you improve your body.

You must not stop there. Improving your mind and spirit will also be huge contributors to your success. The mind is improved with the constant learning of new things, and engaging in work that empowers you. Read for an hour every day and listen to audiobooks, podcasts, videos, and set yourself some mental challenges. Set big goals, it helps to keep the mind active. You may consider learning a foreign language, as this greatly increases mental capacity. The best way to raise our spirit is to remove ourselves from the equation. Do more for others than you do for yourself, and always, always, be a good person and do the right thing. This will uplift your spirit in ways you could never imagine.

Demonstrate Leadership
If you cannot beat them join them, and almost every book on success in the history of books on success talks about leadership. Go back and read that chapter again twice, three times, no matter how many times it takes, learn the LEADERS acronym.

My leadership philosophy will help you tremendously in several parts of your life. If nothing else, always remember that leadership starts on the extra mile. Leaders are the ones who stay back late to make the extra calls. They are the ones that when their work is complete, they spend the extra time mastering their craft. Leaders? Leaders are the ones who disrupt the world with their relentlessness and innovation.

Rise to Challenges
Problems are only problems if we choose to see them as a problem. Within every problem will lie

an opportunity for growth, if you look hard enough. When faced with challenges in the workplace, rise to them. Become a problem solver, and every manager and executive will notice you. The thing is you do not always have to be right and solve the problem. It's the fact that you acted on the initiative to do something about it, instead of sitting at your desk that matters. If you can tackle something big by yourself, I encourage you to do so, even if it is difficult.

You will hear others telling you to over promise and over deliver with your work. My advice would be not to over promise anything unless you are a major league professional. In my opinion, that just sets you up for failure, and you will become overwhelmed with the activities. Instead under promise with what you can do, and make sure you always, always, over deliver. It's what makes the best, the best.

Model the Successful
Every organisation in the world has successful people working for them. Here is the good news, you can find these people and learn what they did to become successful in that organisation, and copy them. This person will be the top producer within their department and are usually results orientated. If you read books on success, you will find that these people usually outperform everyone else by around 20% or more.

Now, it's going to be your job to ask this person, what it is they do, that makes them so successful. Usually, they attribute their success to one or two techniques, and 90% of the time they will share these techniques with you. If they do not? Find someone else that will. You may be wondering why doesn't everyone just ask that person? Here's the reason almost 97% of the people you work with will not ask that question. They will lack the self-awareness to even think of that question. You will be the successful one because you will have asked. Model the successful, and learn how they do their job.

How to be the Best Salesperson
Not everyone is cut out for sales, but those who are can make it big. Every organisation needs a great sales team to be able to stay in business. I could write a whole book on how to become a great salesperson.

However, let me give you a few pointers. Let the prospect do the buying and the selling. Ok, so what do I mean by this? This means that you let them do most of the talking during the sales conversation. Like a great leader, a great sales person is a great listener. As a salesperson, you are always looking to identify what it is your client wants and a way you can fulfil that for them. Treat everyone you have a sales conversation with as a client and be the friendliest person they have ever met, however, always be authentic.

In the sales game, you must be on the ball, common mistakes salespeople make are not knowing enough about their product and overcomplicating it for the client. You need to believe in what you sell, see your product as a solution to client's problems or as a benefit to them. Good salespeople handle objections; great salespeople handle objections before they even arise. It's important to tell the difference between the two. Lastly, always follow up, Zig Ziglar said it best "The fortune is in the follow-up."

In sales you will be faced with more no's than yes's, don't take this personal, keep your goals in mind and your skin thick.

Use Down Time Proactively
When there's not much going on at work, it's easy to be distracted and turn your attention to social media, and have a LOL and a good meme. This just won't cut it in the business world.

However, there are some things that you can do, that will help with your success. Make it your business to follow up on some work related emails. You could check up on others in the office, and see if they need help with anything. Educate yourself on trends that are happening in your industry so that you can anticipate forthcoming changes. Take the time organise your desk, or rewrite your career goals. We all know the power of having our goals written down.

Look After Your Health
I once heard an amazing proverb, "Health is the crown on the well person's head, that only the ill

person can see." What good is it to be the most successful millennial in your organisation if you don't have the health to enjoy it? Stress can have physical implications, so do whatever it takes to minimise stress in your life. So many of us are relying on coffee for our energy these days, but it's much better to get your energy from water so rehydrate yourself by getting your daily recommendation. Did you know that 80% of our brain is made of water? Therefore, it makes perfect sense to me to get plenty of it. We know the implications of smoking and eating unhealthy. Nourish your body with green vegetables, eat protein, and good carbohydrates. Get plenty of exercise, but do not over do it, our bodies will burn out.

We are human beings, not human doings. Small consistent actions lead to the big results. I'm not a health and fitness expert, but I would encourage you to invest in an expert to get the best information you need. The best ones can tell you the quantities of each food you should be eating. Check out www.ProFitness.ie these are the experts on fat loss, and they could help you with nutrition.

Dress for Success
It is sad, but true that the majority of people will judge you based on the clothes you wear. I like to wear Crocs because they are comfortable. Not everyone approves. One morning I came into my cousin's office and had a page on my computer

waiting for me. The page read "Birth control, Condoms 99% effective, The Pill 99% effective, Crocs 100% effective." We all had a giggle in the office that morning.

In Owen Fitzpatrick's book *The Charismatic Edge*, he talks about that how dressing properly makes you more charismatic. In Robert Cialdini's book *Influence*, he discusses how people are more likely to respond, to people who are wearing a well-cut suit versus casual clothes. In my first book, I discuss how dressing appropriately for a college presentation can help you gain extra marks. Therefore, there's a lot to be said about a person who dresses well. I once came across a quote on Facebook that said, "Being poor does not give you an excuse to look poor."

In my opinion, you should dress a little better than everyone else in the office. If you are required to wear a suit, invest in a tailored suit, wear a double cuff shirt with classy cuff links. If you are in a job that is casual dress, I'd go with smart casual. Dress like you are going to meet your worst enemy. I'm a believer in buying good clothes that last. Brooks Brothers shirts are some of the better quality ones, alongside their suits that come highly recommended. I like Levi jeans and Ralf Lauren polo shirts. I find that even after washing them the quality is always there. I think it's wise to dress for the job you want, not the job you have.

Avoid the Brown Nose Trap
For those of you who are unsure as to what a brown nose is. They are the kind of people who lick ass to get their way to the top. The thing is it does work, as executives can be impressed with their stimulating conversation. There is something more powerful that will get you to the most successful position in your organisation. It's when you know the executives by name, and you are seeing going the extra mile to serve them. Don't just talk the talk, walk the talk. In the long run, this will bring you greater success. The brown nose is the one who is constantly trying to impress their superior, by insincerely complementing them and pretending to be something they are not. Remember, always be result and goal orientated, complement sincerely, and be authentic.

If You Have Kids Play with Them
There's a saying that says, "You can choose your friends, but not your family." The Dali Lama says, "Family friends are hidden treasures, seek and enjoy their riches." You hear it so often not to be too busy making a living, that you forget to create a life. That's why it's so important that on your journey to the top, you take the time to play with your kids. Spend time with loved ones, reconnect and resolve conflicts, and avoid future guilt.

Yesterday I was at a yoga class at the Sarasota YMCA, and our instructor took a very spiritual stance even speaking Sanskrit. However, she said something at the beginning of the class that stuck with me, "Life passes us by fast, take time." You can interpret this any way you like. It stood out to me that we only have a short time here with some of our loved ones, and we spend more time with the people we work with than our loved ones. So, take the time to appreciate those you value the most. It's important to you watch your kids grow up, and get in touch with your inner child. Robin Sharma in his book *The Greatness Guide* says, "Take the time to play."

Chapter 9
De Stress More Success

"I've had a lot of worries in my life, most of which never happened."
-Mark Twain

I am by no means an expert when it comes to combating stress. I can only share with you the strategies that have worked for me, and what the real experts are saying on the topic. What I do know is that millennials are the most stressed, depressed and anxious generation of our time. That can be scary and challenging without having a strategy to overcome this stress.

This is a serious epidemic considering that it costs employers $300 billion a year. It's astonishing that up to 77% of people are experiencing physical illness symptoms brought on by stress. Stress is effecting our lives in many other ways, 48% of people lay awake at night because they are stressed. This can't be right, can it? It's even more staggering to think that 54% of people have snapped at a loved one because of stress. Reportedly, 33% of people say that they are living with extreme stress, but what is staggering to me is that 76% attribute their stress to money and work related issues. Let's look at a global statistic, 87% of workers are emotionally disconnected from their work. The scary thing is, that this stress if not dealt with, can lead to all sorts of mental illnesses. That's why I wanted to bring your awareness to this.

Put it Down

I like to use metaphors and relate stories back to college related experiences.

Let's talk about my good friend the professor again. However, this time he doesn't have an empty bucket, but instead he's got a glass of water. While giving a class, he asks the students, how heavy do they think the glass of water is? Their response is somewhere between 100 to 500 grams. The professor says that the weight of the glass is not important, what is important is how long you hold it.

Holding the glass with your arm stretched out for a minute is no big deal. When you hold onto the water with your arm stretched out for an hour your arm will begin to ache. Holding the water with your arm stretched out for a day is going to require medical attention.

The glass weighs the same amount every time, but the longer you hold on to it the greater the burden increases. Sooner or later this burden will become unbearable when all you have to do to release the stress is put the glass down.

Easier said than done I agree but stay with me here, and I'll share actions you can take to put it down. When you put the glass down it is easier to move on in a positive rejuvenated manner. Before you leave work this evening, put the glass down, and leave it behind you. You will feel the weight lifted off your shoulders. Whatever the burden is you are carrying, take a moment to let it go, you can pick it back up again when you are feeling rested and relaxed.

Stress not only causes manifested physical illness, it works in a unique way so that our bodies don't care if it's a little bit of stress over silly things, or a lot of stress over some important factors. When our bodies are faced with a stressful scenario, it represses our immune, and digestive systems and our bodies feel like it must react to immediate danger. What is even more astonishing is that a study by Yale University concluded that our low moods caused by stressed, can negatively influence those around us.

Find Your Tree

Do you know what stress does really good? It's really good at making smart people do stupid things. I don't know about you, but in my opinion, that causes all sorts of problems. The good news is we can control how we react to these situations, and the best time to deal with stress is at the moment it occurs.

Up to 80% of primary care doctor visits are related to stress. However, only 3% are receiving the proper stress management care. That is a scary figure and is why I want to share the techniques in this chapter with you.

I once came across a story of a carpenter, who was doing some restoration work on a barn for a woman. One morning he was late for work due to a flat tire. While on the job, his electric saw stopped working. When it was time for him to go home, his pickup truck wouldn't start. The lady decided to give him a ride home, the entire ride home he was silent. When they arrived at his house before he entered, the carpenter walked over to a tree and touched the branches with both hands. Then they entreated his house, where he turned into an instantly warm and loving husband and father. He walked her back to her car, and curiosity got the better of her, and she asked, "What did you do at that tree?"

His reply, "That is my worry tree."

He said, "I cannot help but have worries on the job, but when I come home in the evening I don't need to bring the worries with me and into my family. So, before I enter the house, I hang my worries upon that tree."

"That is such a great idea." Replied the woman.

"The funny thing is, my worries are nowhere near as big the following day." Said the man softly as he waved the woman off.

The Flight of my Life

I'm both grateful and fortunate to report that I rarely, if ever, find myself stressed. I can honestly say the reason is because I follow the strategies I'm about to share with you. Before we get into it,

I wanted to share with you several scenarios where I could've been stressed, but wasn't.

When I was traveling to visit my cousin Kevin in Florida for a two month vacation and for writer's inspiration. To get there, my flight was from Dublin to Boston with a connecting flight to Fort Myers. It was a Sunday morning and my uncle Derek had given me a lift to the airport early that morning. I decided to check in my luggage and make my way to the US customs clearance area in Dublin. I was flying on September 11th, so the immigration officer was extremely hard on me, and intimidating by asking me what I do for a living, what did my cousin do for a living, and how much money I had on me. I told him my cousin is an attorney, and then he eased up a little bit. This can be stressful for some people as they think they've done something wrong. My thought was that the guy was doing an excellent job and more power to him.

Then I boarded my flight to Boston, and when we landed, I went to the help desk to find out where my connecting flight was located. The lady at the desk asked to see my passport. Of course, I happily obliged as I heard a response from her that would send most people into panic mode 56 minutes before their flight.
"Are you sure you are flying to Fort Myers Sir?
"Yes."
"Are you sure you're flying Jet Blue?"
"Yes."

"Your name does not appear to be on the list."

I looked at her as though she was crazy, and she looked at me as though I was crazy too. I stayed calm while thinking to myself that it could be kind of cool if I had to spend a night in Boston. She proceeded to hand me back my passport as I told her I would go to the gate to see can they help me there.

When I arrived at the gate, I received a similar response. This time the airline personnel wanted to see my flight reference number, which again did not register in their computer system. At this point it was getting closer and closer to the departure time, all I could think was not to worry about events that are outside of my control. This time the guy at the desk was extremely helpful, and before long they had found the issue.

What happened? I was checked in to fly with Aer Lingus to Fort Myers with no connection, they called Aer Lingus and confirmed I was a passenger, so they guy printed me out my boarding pass, and I was good to go. Again, this can pose stress as you may not be getting on the plane. I grabbed me some Dunkin' Donuts coffee and a donut, and I was good to fly. The lady beside me on the plane was amazed at my drive to help people and the potential my first book possesses.

When we arrived at Fort Myers, we walked to the carousel together where we bumped into my cousin Kevin, who is always ready for a good laugh. By most people's standards, I had a pretty stressful day. To top it all off, my bags never showed up on the carousel, and now we had to report to lost luggage.

Here I am, with no clean underwear and wearing jeans in the Florida sun, not a pleasant experience after 14 hours of traveling. Thankfully the airline had located my bag and was to ship it to me the following day. We eventually arrived at our destination, and at this point I was beat up, and just wanted to sleep.

Upon rising the next morning, I discovered that our internet connection was not set up for wireless. How would you react to having no Wi-Fi for two days? To me it was a blessing as I detoxed myself from social media and emails. My point of this story is that when you say calm, hold your nerve, and apply the following techniques you'll be just fine.

What is stress? Where does it exist? Can you touch it? What colour is it? What does it look like? How much time do you spend being stressed? If you weren't stressed how would you spend that time? I believe that most people can't answer the first six questions. However, I bet that you could come up with a lot of answers for the last question. Most of the things that stress us out are of little relevance in the overall greater scheme of things, we take things too seriously and blow them out of proportion.

One of the things that make us stressed is the fear of the unknown. Fear always triggers stress, as we perceive that we are in danger. As humans, we have the need to feel certain. We are never stressed when we have certainty. It's the same when we are worried or nervous about something. I believe the most effective way of dealing with stress that's brought on by fear, is to go out there and face that fear. Feel the fear and do whatever you must do anyway. This may be the point where you say, "I can't do that Gerard I'm too afraid." This is where I say that's ok, let me help you with that.

I want you to think of something that you were once afraid of in the past, and that you no longer fear. How did you do it? What's different this time that you can't do it? I'm here to tell you this time is no different.

I once saw a video online that talked about lobsters, and how they're a mushy animal that lives in a shell. However, the shell doesn't expand. So how does the lobster grow? As the lobster grows, the shell feels very confined, and the lobster becomes stressed and uncomfortable. It then breaks off the shell and goes under the rocks and grows a new shell. Eventually, the lobster will feel under pressure in its new shell, and they repeat the process.

This will happen several times before the lobster is fully grown. What's interesting is the signal for the lobster to grow is that when it feels uncomfortable. If lobsters had doctors, they would never grow. Yet us humans fear this growth so much.

"Our deepest fear is not that we are inadequate. Our deepest fear is that we are powerful beyond measure."
– Marianne Williamson

Times of stress are times for growth, and if we use adversity to our advantage, it can become our greatest gift. Use your stress instead of your stress using you. When you're worried or stressed ask yourself, would a more successful version of myself worry or stress over this?

Test Day

My mother had to go through five weeks of radiotherapy. I decided that I would travel up to the treatment centre with her every day to show my support. Seeing so many people in one room with cancer really helps you put life into perspective. My mother flew through the treatment and didn't let it get her down. Thankfully she has received the all clear from the doctor. Every morning we were collected by a van service that brought us up to the hospital. One morning our van had broken down, and it delayed us over an hour. This is something that would really bother most people, but not my mother.
"What can you do, we'll get there when we get there." She said.
This amazed me because she was so right, complaining about what had happened would

not get us there any faster.

On Friday of that week, we were waiting on the van come, but it was late by around thirty minutes. When it arrived, we got on and were headed for the hospital, a twenty-five minute trip from our house. We were about five minutes away from the hospital when SMACK! A truck rammed into the back of us. We all got some bad whiplash, but the driver really hurt his back. Thankfully nobody was seriously injured. Do you think this is a stressful situation to be in? Of course, it is, most people would be already on the rampage calling the driver of the truck that hit us every name under the sun. What do you think my mother said in this situation?

"It's not that poor man's fault he hit us. He's just an ordinary fella traveling to work just like anyone else, and I'm sure he's in as much shock as us." Was her reaction.

My mother's one of the toughest cookies I know, every day the woman seems to get stronger and stronger. I know that if I have half my mother's strength, I can get through anything. Moral of this story? I'm going to leave that up to your interpretation.

Ok, so let's not beat around the bush any longer. Let's begin to outline the activities you can do to combat stress and reduce the level or cortisol that may be in your body.

Live a Healthy Lifestyle
Here's where I would start, by eliminating toxins in your diet. Food and beverages change the biochemistry of our body; our digestive system is responsible for taking a good chunk of our energy, so when we eat red meat it takes longer for our bodies to digest versus when we eat a salad. My friend Jean-Pierre DeVilliers writes in his book *The Principles of Peak Performance,* that we should eliminate smoking and limit alcohol from our lifestyles.

What a lot of people don't know is that up to 50% of people who are depressed, their depression can be linked to alcohol. Make sure you are getting enough exercise is also a necessity. Little things like getting out for a walk can make a big difference. Be sure also to get enough sleep. If these are areas you are struggling with, be sure to seek help, or pick up a good book on the topic.

Mindfulness
Self-awareness is a subject of exploration in the modern world. When we are self-aware, we can control how we perceive stimuli in the external world. However, self-awareness begins with a transformation of our inner world. You can start this transformation by taking the time for mindful activities, such as meditation and yoga.

Start by meditating 10 minutes a day then build up to a number that feels comfortable to you. On the yoga side of things, this will help you realign your posture into a more natural state and take control of your breathing patterns to give you a boost of energy when needed. I started yoga in Florida, and after the first two classes, I could already see the potential benefits of the practice.

Live in the present moment, forget about the past, forget about the future, focus on being grateful for what you have right now. When I did my podcast with Steven Kotler, we discussed meditation. He told me they did a study of people with Post Traumatic Stress Disorder where the subjects had to mediate. Within four weeks they had drastically reduced their symptoms.

The thing is when it comes to mindfulness most people are doing it wrong. Research from the University of North Carolina discovered that four days of mindfulness training, of just 20 minutes a day was enough to create significant cognitive enhancements. Most people think it's hard to be mindful when in reality it's really simple. Take the time to focus on your breath, when you find your mind wondering that's ok just shift the focus back to your breath.

Be a Human Being
We are human beings, not human doings! What this means is to take time out of each day to perform human activities. Take that extra 10 seconds to hold a door open for somebody, go slightly out of your way to help people when they are in need. This will help you reconnect with

who you are at the core. As human beings, we should be helping each other grow, and not be adding stress burdens or fussing over the possessions of others. Focus on your growth and helping others grow, your whole world will transpire.

Focus on What is Going Right
I went to breakfast this morning with my cousin, that was hosted by an organisation he sponsors. A man was speaking and he said something that prompted my cousin looked at me and say, "Stick that in chapter 9." The man's quote was, "Often our most difficult times are opportunities in disguise." When faced with adversity, focus on what is going right. More than likely you have more than $1 in your pocket, and you can afford to buy yourself something nice. This makes you richer than two-thirds of the world's population. If you are stressed, be grateful for that opportunity. Stress and gratitude cannot happen simultaneously, make sure you choose gratitude every time.

T4M
This little acronym stands for Time for Me and what this means is that every day you take time for yourself. During this time, you do whatever it is you want to do! I know one lady in Florida who takes the time to go horse riding, and my cousin

over there takes the time to play squash. What I like to do is take a nice bike ride listening to some Latin music with the wind at my back or take a walk on the beach. This is much more enjoyable to do in Florida than in Ireland. Do something that gets you excited! Go practice your Spanish on the street with a random person, and you would be surprised as to how much fun you can have.

Chapter 10
Crafting Your Dream Career

"If opportunity doesn't knock, build a door." - Dali Lama

Did you know that 80% of the jobs that gross over $80,000 a year or more, are never advertised? If this does not shock you I do not know what will. Therefore, these jobs are being achieved through promotions or networking. This makes me want to learn how I can get one of these jobs.

You'll need to know how to get into your dream job. I think if you're reading this you want success, and you're an extraordinary person. Why? Because, firstly, you are an action taker. Secondly, you are hungry for success, and thirdly you won't settle for second best. Why should you? We live in a world where success is there for anyone who is willing to do whatever it takes to obtain it.

As a millennial, we are part of a unique club, right now millennials are the biggest generation in the workplace and will soon make up 50% of the entire workforce. However, there's also another unique problem. We are also the generation with the highest amount of unemployment. During this chapter, you will explore choosing the organisation that's right for you. Also, how we can build a career that's in line with our values as human beings.

I don't know what you did or didn't study in college. Maybe you didn't even go to college, that's also perfectly fine. I can only speak for myself, and I studied business. What I've learned is that what you studied may not limit you as much as you think. What these organisations are really looking for is your skill set. They are looking for somebody that will add value to the organisation.

Before you shoot me, let's disclaim the likes of Midwives, Doctors, and general IT specialists. You need a special college degree for those kinds of jobs.

What's really important is your ability to apply yourself and commit in adverse environments that may arise in the workplace. So, keep this in mind when your researching about what your ideal career would look like. An excellent example of this is my cousin in Florida who has his own law firm, so it's logical to think that his employees would come from a law background? Well, you would be wrong to assume this, as one of his star employees has her master's degree in psychology. Right now I'm studying a master's degree in Real Estate and one of the girls in my class studied Social Science and is working in real estate. Another one of the other guys is a qualified school teacher. Maybe you are qualified for your dream job, you just don't know it, yet. On the flip side, some companies accept you for their graduate programmes regardless of academic background.

Researching Your Dream Career

Depending on where you are on the spectrum, I wanted to add this section in for two reasons. The first being maybe you are just out of college, and you're looking to start your career. Second, you are already in the workplace, and you're seeking to change into a job you can inject with your passion.

1. Pick something you can be passionate about.
2. Align your career with your values.
3. Look for growth opportunities.

The Bulletproof Résumé

Where I come from, we call a résumé a CV. This is a document that tells the employer everything they need to know about you before they call you in for an interview. This document contains a list of your work experience, skills, achievements, and a personal mission statement.

The beauty of the résumé is you can tailor it to whatever job you are applying for. There are two things I want to share with you about résumés. Firstly, I was at a mock interview in Dublin, and we were given feedback on the quality of our résumés by an HR professional. You would be surprised to hear what the lady said, that is that 90% of the time the content is

fine, the errors are in the spelling, grammar, and punctuation. Needless to say, you would think that this would be the first thing a person would check before their résumé is reviewed by a potential employer. She said she had one résumé with the paragraphs typed in different fonts and text size. Can you imagine how difficult that would be to read? Never mind hiring this person. I was once at a careers fair when I asked another HR professional, "What does the ideal résumé contain?"
He said, "Google, Elon Musk, 1-page résumé."

When I got home that evening, it was the first thing I did. You should Google it yourself to see how amazing it is, the content is laid out excellently, and is formatted so it's easy to read. One look at his résumé and your first thought is I want to hire this person.

Build Your Personal Brand with Social Media

Getting your name out there is one of the best things you can do to find that dream career. First, determine the value you will bring to organisations. When you have figured out what you stand for as a brand, start providing value and create content. When you have content, and deliver value, it gives you leverage.

The ones with the strongest personal brands are usually industry experts. Becoming an industry expert is no easy task, the best way to become an expert is learn as much as you can.

Read industry reports and talk to people that are making an impact in your industry. Then use your newly found knowledge to publish articles on LinkedIn or maybe even start a blog.

Use social media wisely, be professional and use it as a tool to build your network. Join groups and be proactive in your job search. When connecting with people, always give before you get. This way I promise you that you will receive 10x more in return. Follow companies you see yourself working for so that you receive all the latest news. Get onto LinkedIn use it as an online CV and build that profile!

Career Fairs and Recruiting Events

Even when the job market isn't looking promising, I promise you that there are always job opportunities for those who are willing to up skill to meet the needs of the economy. Those who will put themselves out there and do what it takes to get the job.

This can include networking, and getting your face in front of decision makers. The hardest part is to get your foot in the door. Once you've done that you are a step closer. You could do this by taking a work experience or internship role. Familiarise yourself with job hunting technology. I was at a careers fair, and they had an app that enabled you to upload your résumé, and when you arrived at the event, they handed you a tag.

With this tag, you could touch off a device at prospective employers stands so that you could give them your information via your tag. Apps such as Career Zoo can be tools for you to use to research your career. Social media platforms such as LinkedIn always have job opportunities out there that are tailored towards you and your qualifications. Use these tools to your advantage. You don't know when they will come in handy.

I recommend two things. First, always bring several hard copies of your résumé with you to career fairs. Second, always have an electronic copy saved to your phone so if you ever meet a potential employer and they request your résumé, send it to them right away in front of them. This will demonstrate that you are an action taker, one of the key characteristics 21st-century employers search for.

Interview Preparation and Skills

I've had three formal interviews in my life, so by me telling you what I did is a wonderful indicator of what not to do. However, I can also tell you what I learned, and what I would do next time in order to succeed.

My first interview was at an accountancy firm in Dublin for a job as a tax trainee. I was a good tax student in college, but I was not passionate enough about the subject to pursue a career in that area. However, I figured it could be a good backup if my dream career of writing books and speaking in public didn't work.

It was the morning of my first interview, and I was nervous as hell. Now I'm not someone who gets nervous, but this day I was. When I entered the firm, I felt sick, and I realised straight away that this was not the kind of place I wanted to work. To put it mildly, everyone looked depressed. I was being interviewed by two senior accountants of the firm. One of the interviewers immediately struck me as nervous, but maybe that's just me speculating. The first question he asked me was, "Tell me about yourself."

I said, "I am a passionate, energetic, goal orientated person willing to do whatever it takes to succeed."

Boom! He hits me with, "You sound more like a salesman than a tax trainee."

I knew when he said that, it was game over and I wasn't getting the job. Not that I wanted the job, but that's not the point. Who screws up an interview after 30 seconds? Another question was salary expectations, and I joked a little by saying, "Shall we talk seven figures."

The lady laughed, but the guy broke out in sweats thinking that I was serious. That was the end of that one.

My second interview, funnily enough, was for a competitor's firm. I asked the guy was there any opportunity for me to go from tax into management consulting? His response was, "It sounds to me that you are not familiar with what you want."

I mean I couldn't argue with the guy, but I did know what I wanted, and that was to inject my passion into my speaking and writing career.

My third interview was a sales retention position for a six week summer position, I have read the best sales books on the planet, and I've sold high ticket priced items, and yet these guys still wouldn't give me a job. Was I disappointed? Of course not, if any one of those companies had hired me there is no way I would have written my first book or even to think of writing my second would've been mind blowing.

The point I'm trying to illustrate is authenticity. All of these guys were sharp people. They all said I came across as fully confident, but they could easily tell that my heart wasn't in the job I was interviewing for. The career lady from college once told me that, her advice for people doing interviews was be yourself. The advice she gave me was, "Don't be bold GERARD." I couldn't help it. I just have that level of passion, drive, and entrepreneurial spirit inside me. I can't help but pursue my vision, of what I want my life to stand for.

So, let's get into the tips I can give you to be successful during your interviews. First and foremost, start by doing the opposite of me. Maybe even take a mock interview so that you'll go in with feedback from a professional and with practice and being well prepared.

Dress for Success
Any interview I've had, I always wore a suit. I believe that first impressions make a huge difference, so dress for the job you want, not the job you have. I follow some basic grooming principles making sure my suit is well fitting and clean (Donald in Sarasota can help with this) also wearing a dress shirt buttoned to the top, and a tie that is tied properly. Also, be sure to have your shoes neatly polished. If it's a job where you are not required to wear a suit for the interview, I would almost always wear smart casual. Fellow Irish man Owen Fitzpatrick writes about how dressing properly makes us more charismatic. Buying good quality clothing is an investment, not an expense.

Non Verbal Communication
Watch how you shake hands with the person interviewing you. Being nervous will show in your body language, so try to keep your body in a confident posture. Watch their body language and gestures so you can build rapport with the person you are trying to impress. Show interest in the other person, that you really care about what they are saying to you. Remember if they like you they're equally trying to sell you the job at their company so that you don't go to one of the competitors.

Sell or Be Sold
The interview is the ultimate sales pitch for you to communicate that you're fully competent for the job, and you have what it takes to deliver value to that organisation. You really need to sell yourself. This requires you to be confident, not cocky. Often those who are fully confident are confused with being cocky, but a confident person is just sure of themselves and is fully aware that there are other people out there better than them. So, make sure you convey confidence. The second thing is, if you are strong in a certain area, convey that point to the person interviewing you, they will love hearing about it. You should also make yourself stand out, in a good way, not a bad way like how I did. Read the section on public speaking/presenting this will help you sell yourself more effectively.

Shine Like a STAR
This isn't a framework I came up with, just something I found online, from an unknown source. I think it's pretty cool.
STAR is an acronym that stands for Situation, Task, Action, and Result. You can use this technique in an interview to help you answer questions more effectively. For example, if they ask, "Tell me about a time you demonstrated leadership?"
I think stories are the best way to convey your point to this interviewer. Let me illustrate this for you a little further.

Situation, this is when you outline what you needed to achieve. Let's say that you were the team leader of a project, and it proved to be challenging when it came to getting people engaged. Give an overview, explain that initially people were not willing to listen and nobody was engaging with the work.

Task, this is when the details come in. You want them to understand that when you're presented with a task, you know exactly how to handle it. The task here is that you needed to get people back on track with their task.

Action, here is where the interview gets interesting. Tell the interviewer the actions you took to solve the problem. Right here is your chance to impress the hell out of them. Actions speak louder than words, considering this is something you will have already completed, it shows that you mean business.

Result, I believe that the most important part is not the result, but rather the actions you took. Sometimes, we don't always get our desired outcomes due to unanticipated events. I once came across an excellent quote on change, forgive me for forgetting the actual source, but here it is, "If you focus on results, you never change. If you focus on change, you get the result."

Conclusion
Top Golden Nuggets from the Book

The Bulletproof Mentality

"Whether you think you can or you think you can't, you're right."
- Henry Ford

Challenging times are inevitable for everybody. Having a growth mindset will be the number one tool in becoming the most successful millennial in your organisation. Remember the story of the eagle? He didn't believe in himself. I encourage you to believe in yourself, because if you don't who will? Use the story of the shoe salesmen that went to Africa as a metaphor for what's the best attitude you can have towards work. An attitude of gratitude wins every time. Dare to be different and step outside your comfort zone. Grow every day! Find what's important to you in life and do whatever it takes for you to make it a reality.

Do You Want it? Go Get it!

"If you want to live a happy life, tie it to a goal. Not to people or things."
-Albert Einstein

Studies show that those who have goals, and plans to achieve them, usually do. Go set yourself a BHAG! Everyone I have interviewed on my podcast, any book I have ever read, and interview I have ever listened to all say the same. When you know **Why** you want to achieve something, it always leads to the **How**! Create a vision for what you want your life to stand for, and makes you want to jump out of bed in the morning. Find yourself an accountability partner and check in with them regularly. Always be resilient, success will show up I promise. Sometimes you must fall seven times, just make sure that you get up eight. Have the self-discipline not to eat the marshmallow. I promise your success will taste much sweeter. Then use the CAT method, and I promise you will be successful. If at first, you don't succeed, try and try again. Nothing worth having comes easy.

How to Become a World Class Communicator

"The Single Biggest Problem in Communication, is the Illusion that it has Taken Place."
-George Bernard Shaw

When it comes to communicating so often it's not what we say, rather how we say it that makes all the difference, and the body language we portray. Use the techniques I use when I am presenting, so you can be successful in all your speaking engagements. Always keep it simple and converse with the audience by making them feel you are just like them. Build rapport with people, they will love you for this, and they'll receive the message you are trying to communicate much more clearly. Always see things from the other person's point of view. People have a name for a reason, use it. Never overlook the power of listening, two ears and one mouth. Show interest by asking questions. This will help you in every area of your life, not just the workplace.

The Millennial Leader

"To Lead People Walk Behind Them." - Lao Tzu

Almost 50% of us millennials see ourselves in a position of leadership in the future. That's why I dedicated a whole chapter to leadership. Becoming a strong leader starts as an internal process, then it's an external process. If you want others to follow you as a leader, you need to lead them. The only way to lead is by example. You can't expect others to perform tasks that you are not willing to perform. Become a gardener, set the growing environment so that it's right to plant your seeds. Leaders are humanitarians, who compliment when others criticize, accept while others judge, construct while others destruct, and they give when others take. Remember the LEADERS acronym: Listen, Empathise, Awareness, Decisive, Empower, Relationship build, and most importantly they smile. ☺

Team Work Makes the Dream Work

*"Great things in business are never done by one person. They're done
by a team of people."* - Steve Jobs

We all need to feel like we belong to the team for us to feel fully fulfilled in the workplace. That is why almost 50% of us would give up a portion of our paycheck just to feel connected to a team at work. Remember the story of the All Blacks beating the Irish? What was one of their player's mantras? That's right, champions do more! As a team, we are stronger together. Be sure to always take the point of view of other members into consideration, and there's more than one way to skin a cat. Richard Branson even said it, delegate tasks, nobody is good at everything. Every team needs a clear and common goal that everyone can work toward. When you need everyone to commit to this goal during challenging times, remind them as to why it's important.

What Time is it?

"A man who dares to waste one hour of time has not discovered the value of life."
-Charles Darwin

It's hard to believe that we are interrupted on average every 8 minutes. Be careful not to fall into the time management traps. Avoid being busy for the sake of being busy, instead focus your attention on being productive. We all have the same 86,400 seconds in the day. Some of us use our time better than others. However, people tend to overestimate what they can do in one year, and they underestimate what they can do in ten years. So be patient. Say no to everything that does not bring you closer to your goals. Create a schedule and prioritise the important tasks. Use the Pareto Principle, 20% of our time yields 80% of our results. Have a call to action that makes you get tasks done.

How to Stay Engaged at Work

"Be humble, be hungry and always be the hardest worker in the room."
- Dwayne 'The Rock' Johnson

Staying engaged at work can be challenging at the best of times. That's why it's important to set yourself tasks that you "should do" as a priority, not just tasks you "must do." Find passion and meaning in your work. Don't be afraid to ask for help if you are stuck with something. Avoid negativity and distractions. Recharge the batteries so that you can perform at your peak, rest fuels high performance. Be like former President Obama and nurture your decision ability for the tasks that will keep you engaged. I believe that to be truly focused and engaged, comes from when we feel like we are working towards something that's greater than ourselves. If there's one thing I've learned and that is sometimes we must act our way into feeling, more than we can feel our way into acting.

How to Rise to the Top

*"You will never reach your destination if you stop and throw stones at
every dog that barks."* - Winston Churchill

This chapter was full of golden nuggets that you can use to rise to the top. First, start with having the confidence in yourself that you can succeed. Show up to work early and leave late and be willing to work hard. Stay away from the people that say you can't be successful. Instead, focus your time on improving yourself every day, read books and learn more than anybody else is learning. Become a strong leader and embrace challenges. Learn from people in your organisation that are already successful, ask them how did they do it, use what they did to help you do the same. Dress for the job you want not the job you have. Learn how to become a rainmaker. Fall in love with the process of climbing to the top. However, never forget where you came from, and always make time for what's truly important in life.

De Stress More Success

"I've had a lot of worries in my life, most of which never happened."
-Mark Twain

Just like the quote above, what we worry about most, tend not to happen. However, stress is still a huge epidemic. To many of us lie awake at night not being able to sleep because of stress. Therefore, I felt compelled to help if I could. Remember the story of the carpenter? He didn't bring his worries home. I know it's easier said than done, but it's so important that you do the same thing. When I was traveling to the US I could've got stressed out, but I held my nerve, and it all worked out in the end. Be mindful, take 10 minutes just to breathe and meditate. Try Yoga. It changed my life. When things are going right, celebrate and focus on those things. Take time for yourself, connect with nature, take a walk on the beach. Most importantly we are human beings, connect back to your roots by connecting with those who are less fortunate than you are. I know that you have stress in your life, just remember that there are people that would kill for the life you live.

Crafting Your Dream Career

"If opportunity doesn't knock, build a door." - Dali Lama

Soon millennials will make up 50% of the workforce, time to polish up that résumé. Get out there and meet people that will help you snatch that dream job. Find something that you are passionate about that's in line with your values, and it will be a career that fulfils you. Use social media, career events, recruitment companies, do whatever it takes. I promise that if you're smart about things you'll get an interview with these companies or organisations. Go get a mock interview, and practice and be prepared for the real interview. When it happens, the interviewers will be so impressed. They'll know they've found their candidate. Sell yourself that they'll want to hire you on the spot. Shine like the STAR you are.

About the author

Gerard believes that inside every one of us is unlocked potential. He has made it his mission to help as many people as they can achieve what they want. For the last 10 years Gerard has studied the area of personal development. Having read hundreds of books on the topics and authored some himself, he is a true expert in the field. Gerard is also the host of a podcast show where he regularly interviews experts in their fields. Speaking internationally is something Gerard can put after his name, as he was invited to speak at events in the United States and Spain. He also regularly delivers presentations in companies on topics such as leadership, self empowerment, mindset, and goal settling. For more information about Gerard check out the links below.

Email for interviews and general enquires on booking Gerard to Speak:
info@gerardbissett.com

Books by Gerard: ***The Ultimate Survival Guide for College Success*** Available on Amazon.

Podcast Available on iTunes at:
https://itunes.apple.com/ie/podcast/gerard-bissett/id1146187135?mt=2&ign-mpt=uo%3D4

YouTube for videos and success tips:
https://www.youtube.com/channel/UCgBV6HRXfzxxF1yyJg-XVbg

Facebook for the latest content:
https://www.facebook.com/thehabitsofsuccess/?ref=page_internal

Let's connect on LinkedIn:
https://www.linkedin.com/in/gerardbissett/

Instagram for daily inspiration:
@thehabitsofsuccess

Website for the blog and more information:
www.GerardBissett.com

Resources

Books to Read

Chicken Soup for the Soul by Jack Canfield.
How to Win Friends and Influence People by Dale Carnegie.
Finding my Virginity by Richard Branson.
Made in America by Sam Walton.
Screw It, Let's Do It by Richard Branson.
The Charismatic Edge by Owen Fitzpatrick.
The Gold Mine Effect by Rasmus Ankerson.
The Greatness Guide by Robin Sharma.
The Leader Who Had no Title by Robin Sharma.
The Monk Who Sold His Ferrari by Robin Sharma.
The Power of Habit by Charles Duhigg.
The Power of Positive Thinking by Norman Vincent Peale.
The Quick & Easy Way to Effective Speaking by Dale Carnegie.
Total Recall by Arnold Schwarzenegger.

Acknowledgements

Firstly, I want to thank my mother Grainne. I've been blessed beyond belief to call such an amazing woman my mother.

I would like to thank my cousin Kevin in the United States. You always believed in me, when others didn't. Without your support this book would never of been possible, and for that I am forever grateful. I hope that this book makes you proud.

To my uncle Derek, you have taught me more about business than I ever learned in college. You have given me tremendous support over the years alongside invaluable advice. Thank you for everything you have done I am forever grateful.

To the Declan guy, he's a great guy, believe me. You have always encouraged me to do something that I love. You have also helped me out in more ways than I can thank you for, thank you for your continued support. Great guy folks, great guy...

To Gavin who wrote the foreword to this book. I remember being a school boy watching you on television and saying one day I would be just like you. Thank you for all the help you have given me. Your generosity is inspiring.

To Sharron, the school teacher I never had until I was finished school. You taught me how to construct my writing in a way I never thought possible. I never knew what a compound sentence was until our meetings. Thank you for reviewing my work to ensure that I have no errors.

The my dear friend Gary. He has followed my journey from the start. Thank you for everything buddy, much appreciated.

To my extended friends and family. When I told people, I was going to write a book they didn't believe me. Now that I have written two they ask when's the next one. Thank you all for your support.

To you, yes you, the reader, the listener, the watcher. Without you my dream would not be possible. I want to thank you from the bottom of my heart. If I can help you, let me know!

www.ingramcontent.com/pod-product-compliance
Lightning Source LLC
Chambersburg PA
CBHW030740180526
45163CB00003B/865